WALKING IN YOUR ANOINTING

Knowing That You Are Filled With The Holy Spirit

DAVID E. SCHROEDER

authorHOUSE®

AuthorHouse™
1663 Liberty Drive, Suite 200
Bloomington, IN 47403
www.authorhouse.com
Phone: 1-800-839-8640

First published by AuthorHouse 9/21/2007

ISBN: 978-1-4343-2253-1 (sc)

Library of Congress Control Number: 2007906182
Printed in the United States of America
Bloomington, Indiana

This book is printed on acid-free paper.

David E. Schroeder. Ed. D.
Unless otherwise indicated, Scripture taken from the New
American Standard Bible, Copyright © The Lockman Foundation,
1960, 1962, 1963, 1968, 1971, 1972, 1973, 1975, 1977.

Scripture quotations identified as NIV are from the HOLY
BIBLE: NEW INTERNATIONAL VERSION. Copyright ©
1973, 1978, 1984 by the International Bible Society.

Cover photograph credit: Elizabeth A. Schroeder

DEDICATION

Unlike traditional book dedications, the purpose of this one is not to honor or memorialize a good or great person. It is a dedication not *to* or *for* someone.

Rather, I am dedicating this book *toward* or *unto* a mission that I trust under God it will fulfill – the beckoning of disciples of Jesus to enter into the full awareness and appropriation of the provisions of the Holy Spirit for holy living and empowered service.

I dedicate this book to the purpose of challenging, inspiring and encouraging God's children to walk in their anointing.

Dear children…you have an anointing from the Holy One.
As for you, the anointing you received from him remains in you…
and that anointing is real.
First John 2:18-27

Other Publications By Dr. David E. Schroeder

Solid Ground: Facts of the Faith
Follow Me: Discipleship By the Book
Follow Me Manual
The Centrality of Christ in the Fourfold Gospel (booklet)
Matthew: The King and His Kingdom
The Broken God: Power Under Control
Ephesians: God's Grace and Guidance in the Church
Dadship and Discipleship: Character Where It Counts Most
Pursuing the Glory of God: A Biography of Paul Bubna
Upfront Musings, Christ and Culture on the Campus

For information about Dr. Schroeder's publications, or for ministry inquiries, contact MasterWorks, Inc. by writing to des7340@msn. com.

WHAT OTHERS SAY

There is no subject more important to contemporary Christianity than the person and work of the Holy Spirit. The old saying is still true – "Christianity is hopeless without the Holy Spirit". Dr. David Schroeder masterfully handles the subject in a way that both informs and inspires. You will be blessed by this book!

Jim Cymbala
Senior Pastor,
The Brooklyn Tabernacle

Walking in Your Anointing is a bold and stimulating teaching on the manifestations and filling of the Holy Spirit. This book reveals the transformational journey of Dr. Schroeder as he sought to "redig the wells" of the core values of the early Alliance. Biblical, historical, and personal are descriptions of this work.

Dr. Gary M. Benedict, President
The Christian and Missionary Alliance

Whenever godly leaders point us back to the Holy Spirit, the sweet communion of spiritual intimacy along with the peaceful outcome of good teaching cause us to graduate into a more dynamic level of Christian effectiveness. As I read *Walking in Your Anointing*, Dr. Schroeder's skillful use of the Scriptures, broad personal experience, and sensitivity towards the psychological dynamics surrounding how human beings change moved me to expect more supernatural activities of the Holy Spirit in my own life and ministry. It will have the same impact on you.

David D. Ireland, Ph.D.
Senior Pastor of Christ Church, Montclair, NJ & Author, *Journey to the Mountain of God*

This is a well written book and manual for seekers of the fuller Christian life, providing answers many of us have on the things of the Spirit. The author has taken the balanced approach of combining careful biblical exegesis with corresponding personal experience, and in so doing has helped to clear up the confusions between the baptism and the filling of the Spirit; as well as the manifestations and the gifts of the Spirit. Christians from different cultural or theological backgrounds can benefit greatly from reading this book.

Abraham and Lillian Poon
Pastoral Leadership Team
San Jose Christian Alliance Church

David Schroeder has forged a middle path and a bridge between charismatics and evangelicals. *Walking in Your Anointing* provides a vital balance by encouraging open expectation of the supernatural with discernment and without fear. It gives sound counsel for the higher and deeper life of the Spirit that God desires for every believer.

Paul L. King, D.Min., Th.D.
Faculty Coordinator, Diploma of Theological Studies
Assistant Professor of Theology, School of LifeLong Education
Oral Roberts University

This is a book that will create a hunger in your heart for more of Jesus. If you have ever sat in church service in North America and thought to yourself, 'There has to be more than this," then this is a book you need to read. David Schroeder is my dear friend and beloved colleague in ministry. He not only writes about the Spirit-Filled life, he lives it and models it for the next generation. Come Holy Spirit!

Dr. Ron Walborn
Professor of Pastoral Theology
Nyack College

After more than 20 years of Kingdom service in multiple cultural settings, I see two indispensable components to fruitful life and ministry: knowing our positional authority in Christ and moving in the unction of the Holy Spirit. These two deeply theological and experientially appropriated realities turn mere people into dynamic advancers of the Kingdom of God. David Schroeder offers us an insightful, biblical and fresh look at Holy Spirit anointing. I recommend this book to anyone needing a fresh outpouring or reinvigoration of power for life and service.

Rev. Chuck Davis
Senior Pastor
Stanwich (CT) Congregational Church

Somewhere I have heard, "Mystery is not the absence of reality. It is the presence of more reality than we can bear." Should we be surprised that when God's Holy Spirit is unleashed in ours, it would have consequences that are marvelous, miraculous and mysterious? Based on research, Scripture and personal experience, Dr. Schroeder's book presents a thorough understanding of how we can know that the Holy Spirit is at work in us.

Stephen E. Freed
International Director
International Teams

I want to highly encourage hungry hearted pastors and laypeople to get their hands on this book. As a pastor in the Christian and Missionary Alliance for over twenty years, I've preached on the filling of the Holy Spirit and recently was able to weave key aspects of David's book into my messages. Not only does his book renew a desire to seek God for His fullness in our lives and reassure us that we can know we are filled but it also will help us recover our spiritual heritage in the C&MA. David steers a biblically balanced and sensitive course between charismania and the charismaphobia - no easy task! Get this book and hoist the sail of your heart for the Wind of the Spirit!

Pastor Brad Bush
Pastor, Maple Ridge Community Church
West Lafayette, Indiana

BIOGRAPHICAL SKETCH FOR DR. DAVID E. SCHROEDER

Dr. David E. Schroeder has recently been called to be the president of Somerset Christian College in Zarephath, New Jersey, a new college that is being built on an old foundation known as Zarephath Bible Institute. Serving the next generation within a context of spiritual renewal, ethnic diversity, and Christ-centered higher education has been his passion for over thirty years.

Prior to this calling, Dr. Shroeder was president of International Teams, a nondenominational evangelical mission agency, headquartered in Elgin, Illinois.

A 1968 graduate of Nyack College, Dr. Schroeder was ordained in 1974 by The Christian and Missionary Alliance, the parent denomination of the college, founded by Dr. Albert Benjamin Simpson. A St. Paul, Minnesota native, Dr. Schroeder has pastored churches in the United States and planted a church in Wokingham, Berkshire, England. In addition to his B.A. in philosophy, Dr. Schroeder earned the M.A. in humanities from Manhattanville College, the S.T.M. from New York Theological Seminary and the Ed.D. from New York University.

His experience includes serving as VP for US Ministries for Trans World Radio from 1982-87, Executive Vice President and then President of Philadelphia Theological Seminary from 1988-91, and Director of Higher Education for The Christian and Missionary Alliance from

1991 until 1993 when he assumed the presidency of Nyack College. He was elected to serve also as President of Alliance Theological Seminary beginning in September 2000.

During his administration, the student population of the college and seminary more than tripled. The Manhattan campus, a product of Dr. Schroeder's vision, began offering full degree programs in 1997, and today serves over 1,200 students.

He has served as a board member of Atlantic Bridge, Overseas Ministry Study Center, The Christian and Missionary Alliance, Christian Herald, International Teams, Willow Valley Retirement Communities, The C&MA Fund, The Malachi Fund, and Arise and Walk Ministry Foundation.

A frequent speaker at men's retreats, mission conferences, and seminars, David Schroeder's recent international ministries include Nigeria, the Philippine Islands, China, Lebanon, United Kingdom, Russia, Holland, Ukraine, Thailand, South Korea, Peru, Costa Rica, Ecuador and Argentina.

In 1987 Dr. Schroeder began MasterWorks, Inc., a ministry that produces, distributes and teaches discipleship materials, featuring his book *Follow Me: Discipleship By the Book* and the *Follow Me Manual*. Over 700 churches and men's groups have used this material.

He is married to Betzi, and they have three grown children; Christine, Matthew and Brian, and four grandchildren.

CONTENTS

ACKNOWLEDGEMENTS

A book of this nature is not simply a project that is next in line in an author's to-do list. Nor can its substance be merely the product of current thinking. Learning to walk in the Spirit, hungering for daily filling to minister out of anointing is a spiritual aging process – the fermentation of the soul – that only God can bring about in His time and way.

So, first acknowledgments must be directed to our tri-personed God –Father, Son, and Holy Spirit – whose creative work gives the possibility, the hunger and the conditioning for receiving His fullness.

Furthermore, learning about the anointing of God cannot happen in isolation. In the community of God's people we grow into His likeness, as reflections of His Being laser us from all the gifts and manifestations of our brothers and sisters. And the Spirit-carriers who have impacted me are too numerous to mention. Nevertheless, in this craving after fullness that has been the dominant part of my life for the past decade, several individuals have encouraged me greatly, and I would be remiss not to mention them.

Two huge influences are like Abel (Hebrews 11:4); though being dead they yet speak. Both are luminaries in the history of the denomination of my heritage: Drs. A. B. Simpson and A. W. Tozer. They were modern pioneers in the Spirit whose writings have etched a view of God in my heart. Of quite different dispositions, this they had in common – a voracious appetite for experiencing the fullness of God in their lives.

Colleagues and prayer partners in various stages of my life have also impacted me greatly; specifically I recall Brian Mills in the UK, Bruce Bliss, Stephen Freed—these three taught me not to fear emotional response to the Holy Spirit. Abraham and Lillian Poon, Ron and Wanda Wallborn, Chuck and Ingrid Davis, walked with me as I learned to walk in spiritual confidence. And hundreds of young worshipping warriors at Nyack College over a period of twelve years taught me about joy and abandonment in God.

To Dr. Paul King, Assistant Professor of Theology at Oral Roberts University, I owe both a cognitive and emotional debt. Dr. King's thorough research of the history of The Christian and Missionary Alliance, chronicled excellently in his recent book *Genuine Gold*, corroborates much of the pneumatology I present in this book, and his courage to remind Alliance people of their heritage is inspiring.

Of huge help in sharpening my thinking and presentation in preparing this book has been my sister Dr. Diane Zimmerman, whose own growth in the pneumatic was a delightful surprise as we delved into the theology of the Spirit. Also, I am deeply grateful for the cheerful and expert help given so often by my assistant at ITeams, Dianne Clark.

Finally, I am thrilled to be finding so many of my current colleagues in International Teams, in the USA and around the world to be walking in their anointing.

To all of these and hundreds of others, I am most grateful.

PREFACE

Writing about the person and work of the Holy Spirit is like trying to describe all the weather patterns around the world while sitting in a Manhattan office without a view. The Wind blows where He wishes, and *you cannot tell where it comes from or where it is going* (John 3:8). Or it's like trying to see the vastness of the universe with only the naked eye. The forty billion-plus galaxies defy comprehension, let alone description. Even so, the workings of God's Spirit are so vast, so complex, and so mysterious that we can only point to specific activities that are clearly His doing and say, "That must be the work of the Holy Spirit."

When we see such an activity or experience His presence and power, there is no doubting, but because those instances seem so rare for many Christians, we want to attribute other stirrings to Him, which we are not sure are His. So much do we long to demonstrate spiritual power and effectiveness that we assume the least gentle breeze is the Holy Spirit. To be sure, sometimes God reveals Himself quietly and gently, but never without manifest assurance that it is He.

The primary thesis of this book is that the baptism of the Holy Spirit is a definite act of God subsequent to a believer's conversion, and that many further fillings of the Spirit will occur. The key to the Spirit-baptized believer walking in empowered confidence is having received an evidence or manifestation of the Spirit's initial filling. Some groups have insisted that the only evidence is speaking in tongues, but a careful look at Acts reveals that sometimes the Lord gave other manifestations to assure the believer of the Spirit baptism.

The Christian book market offers many "How to be filled..." books with varying prescriptions. Maybe you have read some of them. These are helpful, but can be confusing. It's like having a dozen sets of instructions for putting together a bicycle. The parts are all there, but unless you know what goes where and in what order, you may end up with something quite other than a bicycle. But the Holy Spirit's filling is not a tangible product; He is like a wind,[1] and His effects cannot be manufactured or predicted. They can be and should be experienced, however, by every believer. The good news is that if you are filled with Him you will have assurance of the Holy Spirit's manifest presence and we will know it. A. W. Tozer rightly wrote:

Neither in the Old Testament nor in the New, nor in Christian teaching as found in the writing of the saints as far as my knowledge goes, was any believer ever filled with the Holy Spirit who did not know he had been filled. Neither was anyone filled who did not know when he was filled. And no one was ever filled gradually. The man who does not know when he was filled was never filled (though of course it is possible to forget the date). And the man who hopes to be filled gradually will never be filled at all.[2]

INTRODUCTION

Surprised by the Spirit

Never in my wildest imaginations would I ever have thought that I would write a book about the filling of the Holy Spirit or attempt to impart an understanding of His activity in and through Spirit-filled believers. God knows how frustrated, threatened and turned off to this issue I have been for most of my Christian years. I have been comfortable writing about spirituality in a more general sense, such as discipleship. But just as C. S. Lewis was *surprised by joy*,[3] so have I been surprised by manifestations and fillings beyond what my theology allowed. So, I write somewhat autobiographically out of the surprising, abundant blessing that I once spurned. And I would imagine that every card-carrying evangelical Christian might be so blessedly surprised if our doctrine and paradigm did not unnecessarily limit the work of the Spirit in our lives and in our churches.

I am impelled to write this book for believers who are seeking to live a more empowered life, but who are paralyzed by the confusion and imprecision of so many voices. Traditionalists, evangelicals, charismatics, and Pentecostals see the work of the Holy Spirit in different ways. My approach is not to start with a theological banner to uphold, but to deal honestly and with the relevant biblical texts and invite true seekers to receive the Spirit's fullness. Many of these, I hope, will be my kinsmen in the faith, members of The Christian and Missionary Alliance, who have such a rich spiritual heritage buried beneath decades of pneumaphobic[4] dust.

1

But I also write to unify the Church on an issue that has needlessly divided the evangelical church.[5] Many individuals and churches that hold to basic, biblical convictions withhold fellowship from other parts of Christ's body because of differing ideas of the work of the Holy Spirit in the lives of believers. For years I contributed to this unnecessary fissure. I have come to see, however, that this problem largely exists because we have not paid adequate attention to nuances in Scripture. For example, the church denomination in which I serve, The Christian and Missionary Alliance, has no shortage of books about the Holy Spirit. Indeed, our founder A. B. Simpson was prolific in his writing about the divine third person.[6] Nevertheless, I believe that at a critical juncture in its history the Alliance might have responded better and more biblically to the challenge of some of the pentecostally inclined brothers and sisters, and perhaps would have avoided much tension and division.

The early days of many evangelical movements were pioneering, radical, pneumatically charged, and independent of ecclesiastical expectations. Leaders championed their vision without worrying about anything other than being biblically faithful for the glory of God. In the last decades of the nineteenth century and early years of the twentieth century people who associated with these movements were fearlessly open to workings and manifestations of God in His Trinitarian provisions of grace. Those early days were reminiscent of Jeremiah 2:2, 3:

> *I remember concerning you the devotion of your youth,*
> *The love of your betrothals,*
> *Your following after Me in the wilderness,*
> *Through a land not sown.*
> *Israel was holy to the Lord,*
> *The first of His harvest...*

Alas, for Israel, and for many evangelicals, those early experiences did not endure. Predictably and maybe inevitably, formality and normalcy set in as the movement aged. Doctrines were formalized, policies were set, manuals were written, and a respectable, predictable theology became acceptable, often as compromises or moderations of positions inimical to institutional respectability. But with all of that, one suspects that many evangelicals have thrown out the pearl with the shell. When the Pentecostal movement was re-ignited in the first decade of the twentieth century, much of the Church was not willing to embrace the new energy because that movement came with some undesirable baggage—the insistence that tongue speaking was the only sign of being filled with the Holy Spirit. Unfortunately, a stand had to be taken, and maybe the line was drawn too firmly and too exclusively.

Releasing the Spirit

Another purpose for this book is my hope to encourage biblical Christians to reclaim our birthright. I believe that modernism has diluted our theology and experience of the Holy Spirit. The effect of this is a disempowered clergy and laity within many churches. Inadequate pneumatology has left the church divided and many Christians spiritually impotent. By settling for a "just-take-it-by-faith" pneumatology, we are depriving our children and ourselves of part of the glorious heritage of followers of Christ. So I write to contribute to a broader understanding of the Spirit's work and to encourage a greater openness to fillings and manifestations of the Spirit in our lives and ministries.

My interests, however, are not merely personal or pragmatic. They are also biblical. I had been taught that the Gospels, Acts and Epistles do not share a common view on the work of the Holy Spirit. The Gospels, so this line goes, are pre-Pentecostal, and, therefore, we cannot expect their references to the work of the Holy Spirit to be relevant to our day. Acts, I was taught, is historical, not doctrinal, so it would be dangerous to draw any conclusions about the workings of the Holy Spirit from that historically unique epoch. Only the Epistles, I learned, would be useful for developing an adequate pneumatology for believing, teaching and experiencing. While certainly we cannot reduce the Holy Spirit to doctrine, we are surely justified in releasing Him from the strictures of the segmented, dispensational understanding I had been taught. Are we quite sure we have seen all He plans to do in, for and through the Church? Are there no "latter day rains" yet to experience?

A decade ago or so, as I pondered the missionary passion to "bring back the King" by fulfilling the Great Commission, I sensed the Lord asking me a very intimidating question, "David, do you think if all My people followed your brand of Christianity that the job would ever get done?" It was a question whose answer was assumed in the asking. I realized that if it depended on my generic brand of faith Jesus would never return. Something a lot more radical is demanded. And, praise God, something a lot more radical is being practiced by millions of disciples in this country and even more so in other nations. And I wanted in on the action. So, I went back to Scripture to re-evaluate some of my preconceptions.

I have come to see a wonderful coherence in the Spirit's workings throughout Scripture. Yes, there are different vocabularies used by different authors, but by ignoring important nuances in critical passages such as 1 Corinthians 12 we have clouded the issues and unwittingly sparked battles of "friendly-fire" within the body of Christ. So, part of this book will be an examination of key texts to demonstrate the coherence of Scripture on the topic of the filling of the Holy Spirit. It is my great hope that for those who have too little of what they believe others have too much, a new experience with the Holy Spirit will ensue. And it is my great hope that those who believe they "have it" will come to see that what they have may be different than what they think they have or could have.

Spiritual Confidence

I have also come to believe that God loves boldness. I know He loves brokenness, but I think He also loves boldness because it is through boldness that faith is expressed. (In fact, that is the only explanation I can find for the Lord's favor seemingly resting on the ministries of some Christian media celebrities whose private lives are far from Christ-like.) When the Apostle Peter was filled with the Holy Spirit (see Acts 4:8, 31), he became bold in his faith and witness in a transforming way. In a sense, it is newly received boldness that enables me to write this book, because as I confess in Chapter One for nearly a half century I lived as a pre-Pentecostal Christian. Like Apollos in Acts

4

18, I functioned in ministry through my own gifting, not through the Spirit's empowerment. This is not to say I was not serving as a disciple of Jesus Christ, but as I found out, I had segregated the persons of the Trinity, as many evangelicals seem to do. Chapter Two demonstrates the unity of the Trinity in all the work of God. We need not fear that we are slighting Jesus by seeking the filling of the Holy Spirit, as the first generation of disciples would learn.

Today, however, many Christians are more like uninformed Apollos or timid Timothy than bold Peter. We lack spiritual confidence. In fact, many Christians suffer from spiritual inferiority complexes—an idea we will explore together in Chapter Three.

A major burden behind this book is to help recover the bold, aggressive, courageous witness that the Church once knew. When we think of "bold, aggressive, courageous witness" today, we think of Muslims, not Christians. And they don't even have the Holy Spirit! Imagine if followers of Jesus around the world evangelized with the same boldness as the early church did!

Chapter Three seeks to show that spiritual as well as physical baptism is intrinsically linked to discipleship, as described in the Great Commission.[7] This early reference to being baptized in the Holy Spirit was given by Jesus Himself and provides continuity between the Gospels and the Book of Acts. In Chapter Four we note many biblical examples of individuals and groups who received the affirmation of manifestations of the Spirit—sometimes "tongues," but more often, other manifestations.

Exploring "Things of the Spirit"

Chapter Four looks closely at manifestations of the Spirit, especially those listed in 1 Corinthians 12, where the Apostle Paul urges his spiritual children not to be ignorant of "things of the Spirit" (verse 1; *pneumatika)*. We also see the fruit(s) of the Spirit of Galatians 5 as manifestations of His transforming power in the life of Spirit-filled believers. We move, then, in Chapter Five to the topic that, in my opinion, has paralyzed and confused the study of the work of the Holy Spirit, namely, the spiritual gifts, or the *charismata*, as they are commonly called. This chapter is quite different than the big catalog of "gifts" that many others have written about.

Having made the point that gifts are given at the time of regeneration (but often not activated until later) and that manifestations give evidence of the baptism and filling of the Holy Spirit, in Chapter Six we invite the reader to "enter in" and receive all the fullness of God. Chapter Seven tells the stories of how twenty-two Christians, whom I surveyed, appropriated the filling of the Holy Spirit. So, that's the architecture of this book.

All authors bring their own "baggage" and life context to their writing. In my case, while I have written this book for all Christians, my own denominational roots give the context. Dr. A. B. Simpson's influence on my life has been enormously profound, and my personal and professional involvement with the movement he started, The Christian and Missionary Alliance,[8] gives me a vantage point for looking both directions—toward evangelical and Pentecostal traditions.[9]

Regardless of where you stand on this issue now or how you react to the ideas herein presented, please understand that this book is not written to fuel the debate, but to recover a waning legacy of evangelical believers. In "re-digging the wells" of our heritage, we must recover not just correct biblical pneumatology, but also our passion for the fullness of Jesus and the Holy Spirit.

CHAPTER ONE:
FROM RELIGION TO REVELATION

I'm what they call "blue-blood Alliance." My parents carried me to Simpson Memorial Church of The Christian and Missionary Alliance in St. Paul, Minnesota from my earliest days. Being first-generation Christians they were both very enthusiastic about their faith as they grew under the preaching of such great pastors as Reverend Paul Kenyon, and Pastor C. J. Mason at Simpson and later by pastors Tracey Miller and James E. Davey at Camp Hill, PA.

At the age of four in a Child Evangelism Fellowship meeting in our back yard (so my Mom later told me, as I have no memory of this whatever), I responded to a message of the "Wordless Book," and asked Jesus to forgive me of my sins and come into my heart as Savior. This experience must have been real because within a few years I was "saving my friends" by actively witnessing. Some of this witness, I confess, was motivated by wanting to ascend the rankings ladder within Sky Pilots and later Boys Brigade.

In my first year as a teenager, my family moved to Camp Hill when my Dad became General Manager of Christian Publications, Inc., the publishing house of the C&MA. This was a traumatic move for me. The teenagers in PA were far more advanced in their practice of carnality than my peers in Minnesota. Wanting to be accepted by the in-crowd, and being subject to the surging hormonal awakening of all teenage boys, I soon lost all sense of my commitment to Christ. However, I faked it pretty well.

A pretty severe back injury playing football in my sophomore year sidelined me from my god—Sports—and forced me to examine my not-so-Christian life. A Youth For Christ director moved into town and virtually coerced me to assume leadership of a YFC Club he wanted to start in our school. Thankfully, the meetings would not start in the school building. Unthankfully, they would be in my house, and the only other ones interested were a dozen junior high girls. With my parents' full approval, I became president of the YFC Club, a position that for me lasted three more years. Looking back, clearly this was God's way of getting me back on track and declaring myself as a Christian in my high school. Soon I was leading others to Christ, and the Club flourished.

Wholly Sanctified

During one of the Youth For Christ Christmas Holiday Retreats, held in Bethlehem, PA, an old-time Alliance preacher named Reverend Roy Wilson from Washington, (Western) Pennsylvania, was the featured speaker. He introduced us to the work of the Holy Spirit, and I spent many hours late one night emptying myself of sin so that the Holy Spirit could fill me. Then triumphantly I returned home and announced to my parents that I was now fully sanctified. And I was! — for about a day. I learned two things from that experience: the Holy Spirit wants to fill us for holy, effective lives, and it doesn't happen all at once. This latter idea would be both helpful and hindering to me in years to come.

By my senior year, 1963-64, I was sure I would need spiritual empowerment because I would be going to the United States Military Academy at West Point. Having been chosen Keystone State Boys Representative from my high school, I attended a summer "boot camp" at Penn State University, and was virtually assured a nomination to become a cadet. I was not enamored by the prospect of a military career, but I was prey to the sense of being so honored that the decision was not one that I wanted to submit to God. But he intervened. In filling out the application forms, I noticed a prohibition against anyone who had uncontrollable allergies. This certainly applied to me because every fall, despite taking many medications and getting weekly injections, my nose was like Niagara, my eyes felt like poison ivy, and my sneezing was nearly volcanic. So certain had I been that I would be going to West Point that I didn't apply to any other college. When I found I did not qualify for being a cadet, I begrudgingly assented to applying to the college from which my sister had just been graduated—Nyack Missionary College, just a few dozen miles down-river from West Point.

While my spiritual life was not stellar at Nyack College, the biblical, theological and liberal arts education I gained was outstanding. Some of the professors had a huge impact upon me, both academically and spiritually. Perhaps the peak of my spiritual experiences at Nyack was the Spiritual Emphasis Week ministry of Dr. Stephen Olford. His emphasis on the sacrificed life led me to make a commitment for service that has been upon me ever since. I remember him speaking so vividly about the tongs used by the priests to hold the sacrifices on the burning altar. One part of the tong he called Discipline; the other he called Dedication. I went forward, seeking to present myself as a living sacrifice to God.

During the summers of my college years I worked for my Dad, setting up the bookstores at Alliance camps and selling all kinds of books and "holy hardware" to the campers. I had hundreds of hours to read, and often my choices were the Puritan and Reformed writers of centuries ago. One year when Dr. Harold Walker of the Missionary Church was the evening evangelist, I was so moved by a sermon on the filling of the Holy Spirit that I went forward to seek that filling. I remember praying for a while, but when nothing happened (I didn't know what I was to expect), I just went back to the bookstore to sell more books.

Generic Is Good Enough For Me

During my senior year at Nyack, I was filling out a pre-service application form when I was confronted by this question: *Will you teach the necessity of the filling of the Holy Ghost as a definite act subsequent to salvation?* Now, I wanted to be approved for service, and I knew what answer the Alliance officials wanted. However, I had also developed a theology of process regarding sanctification, and I saw no difference between that and baptism or filling of the Spirit. We had gone over the crisis versus process ideas in class, and since my experiences up to that point showed no perceptible results from seeking the filling of the Holy Spirit, I assumed the question was really asking about sanctification. An older friend advised me that if I had to give an answer I knew they didn't want, I should answer as briefly as possible. So I just wrote "NO."

That began a series of letters between Alliance "headquarters" and me, from which I felt demeaned and in which I acted superior. I actually began to wonder whether the Alliance deserved me. Having also been hypercritical of A. B. Simpson's anemic theology, as I then saw it, I was quite sure I would not pursue a ministry in the denomination founded by him.

In those days the Alliance didn't have a seminary, so I didn't have to choose not to go to it. Rather, my young bride Elizabeth and I gladly headed west to my roots, St. Paul, where I enrolled in Bethel Theological Seminary. We loved it there, but two factors caused us to leave after one year: I was quite sure I didn't want to be a pastor, and my Dad had just lost the sight of his second eye. He was legally blind—not at all a good situation for a publisher. So we moved back to Pennsylvania where I became his eyes, sales manager and editorial assistant. During those three years, 1969-72, we saw the Lord miraculously heal my father, I gained invaluable experiences in leadership and management, we worked as youth directors in our church, and we had our first child, Christine. Elizabeth also miscarried a daughter she named Rebecca Joy.

During those years my views on the Holy Spirit didn't change much, but I became a voracious reader of apologetics, especially C. S. Lewis and Francis Schaeffer. In college I had majored in philosophy, focused on Soren Kierkegaard, and declared myself to be a Christian existentialist. Schaeffer's Upper Story / Lower Story argument in *Escape From Reason* convinced me that experiential faith (not that I had much) was an inadequate base for a belief system. I was now properly *generic evangelical*, much like the Alliance. We were respectable, predictable, and denominational. Hallelujah! Oops, I mean, Amen!

Coming Closer To God

Then came my Call. After three years of peddling products, I grew restless. At a business education seminar at a posh hotel in New York City, I inadvertently led a man to faith in Christ. Doug was a lapsed Roman Catholic and a cost accountant of a NYC bank. He lived in Westchester County, and his marriage was falling apart. His priest had not been able to help him. As we talked, I was able to respond to his questions with Scripture. He was amazed that the Bible had something relevant to say. He knew that Vatican II had recently made it legitimate for Roman Catholic lay people to read Scripture, but was quite sure he wouldn't understand it. I led Doug through a prayer of repentance, and suggested he and his wife should find a good biblical church.

When I returned home, I asked whether there were any good Alliance churches in his area of Westchester. To my amazement, I learned about an exciting new work in Armonk that was built by the new, home-Bible-study movement. Many Catholics had come to faith in these groups, so my friends would fit in. So, having called Doug and having told him about Hillside Church, my responsibility for him was done.

A few months later I attended the C&MA Annual Council with my Dad and others to sell books. Casually, a guy walked up to me on the last day and introduced himself as Roland Coffey, pastor of Hillside Church in Armonk. He said that he had met Doug, had been looking for me all week, and now he had a wonderful plan for my life. His church had a large youth group, led by two faithful lay people. The church wanted to hire an assistant pastor for youth. I thanked him for the offer, explained I needed to stay with my Dad (even though his sight had returned), and thought my future was in business.

The next day found me closer to God than I had ever been, flying on the inaugural flight of a Boeing 747 from San Francisco to Chicago, en route to Harrisburg. Somewhere about 35,000 feet above sea level, the Lord revealed to me very clearly that He was calling me to Armonk. Gingerly, I told my Dad about the talk with Reverend Coffey, and wondered what he might think about my considering the offer. Wisely, he asked whether I had any sense of God's leading about this. I told him I had more than a leading; I had a call. He said to pursue it, and if God was behind it, by all means I should go. Later he told me he always knew I should go into ministry in the church, even though he and his board were hoping I would be his successor at CPI.

Two years of romping with the youth were highlighted by an extended series I taught on "What It Means to Follow Jesus," an examination of the discipleship passages in the gospels, which later became the foundation for my doctoral dissertation and the book *Follow Me*. For a few decades I actually believed that this character-based approach to spirituality was the final word. Wasn't it right from the mouth of Jesus?

After two years, Pastor Coffey accepted a call to a church in Florida, so after hearing a few candidates for the senior pastorate, the elders said to me, "We're willing to take a chance on you if you're willing to take a chance on us." I was willing, and thus began four years of ministry in a multi-ethnic, multi-theological, multi-economic, and multi-denominational church. And little did I know I was walking right into the jaws of a surging charismatic movement in the mid-1970s.

Comfortably Uncharismatic

Preaching came relatively easy to me, having had a good biblical education at Nyack. But pastoring was very difficult. And the pastoral needs in the Armonk church were abundant, what with many new believers—especially women whose husbands were not saved. We also had many charismatic sympathizers, including some of the church fathers. Exacerbating the situation was a nearby Episcopal church undergoing renewal led by a very charismatic, in every sense of the word, priest. Many of my members frequented his noontime, weekday services. Although they said nice things about my sermons, there was always an underlying discontent and disappointment. Also the Alliance church in an adjoining town featured a ministry to young singles, which was led by some really outlandish worship leaders. We attended every so often, and always came home angered and threatened by their charismania.

Because both these groups—the charismatically inclined members and the young singles—talked often about hearing from God and showed belief in the "sign gifts," I countered by inviting a well-known theologian from the Alliance's new seminary to speak at our church on the issue of "special revelation." He assured us all, and greatly relieved me by doing so, that God's revelation ceased with the closing of the canon of Scripture, and the most we can expect today is general guidance as we read the Word.

Thus, I settled into a comfortable generic evangelicalism, ordained to the ministry of the Christian and Missionary Alliance on April 19, 1974. We built a new church facility in Armonk, and I was eager to prove myself to be a good pastor/preacher. But in my soul I was aware of spiritual and emotional blockage. My worship was sterile, my witness was tentative, and my leadership was formulaic. Even my hope of being sanctified—by process, of course—was dashed by ugly interior characteristics I tried to hide: sins like pride, materialism, wrongful ambition, lust, rebellion, and self-centeredness. Above all, though, I was entrenched in dogmatic assurance that my theology was *kosher*.

All these wonderful attributes I took with me into the next five phases of ministry. As Associate Pastor for Adult Teaching Ministries at Long Hill Chapel in Chatham, New Jersey, I found myself in a wonderful congregation of mostly upper-middle class, sophisticated suburbanites, though a small minority of financially challenged members attended the church. Though the church was known for its compassionate outreach to nursing homes, asylums and homeless missions, the Chapel was clearly a generic evangelical church in its understanding of the Holy Spirit.

Under the good leadership of Pastor Paul Bubna, the pastoral staff taught a Sunday Night series on the gifts of the Holy Spirit, which I had orchestrated based on teachings I had largely received at a Bill Gothard seminar. The teaching focused on gifts that are imparted at conversion and become operational upon being discovered and used in ministry. Excluded from the teaching is an emphasis on experience with the Holy Spirit in being filled and the prospect of receiving manifestations of the Spirit.

The Yankee Charismatic

An unexpected encounter with a C&MA leader at the InterVarsity Urbana Conference in 1979 resulted in an overseas appointment for us. During our two year ministry with the C&MA in England, ironically, I was known as the charismatic pastor in town, simply because we attended the monthly renewal meeting in the town hall. We also attended an ecumenical house fellowship that leaned toward charismatic experience, but we were busy building an Alliance church and not wanting to embroil it in controversy. I preached the gospel and on the nature of the Church. The ministries of Pastors David Watson, Michael Green and David Pawson impacted me in a pro-charismatic way during those days. But the most lasting spiritual experience of England for me was the deep *koinonia* I experienced for the first time, by meeting daily at 6 a.m. with five other guys. We sang, we worshipped, we prayed, we cried, we laughed, we dreamed, and we imparted the blessing of the Holy Spirit into each other. The spiritual imprint of fellowship with Brian (Brethren), Eric (Pentecostal), Jim (Methodist), John (Roman Catholic), and Ian (Methodist) is still tattooed on my soul as evidence that bonding of Spirit-filled men is truly transformational.

Returning to the USA, I joined the leadership team of Trans World Radio. During that five-year ministry, I gained a heart for the world, and from extensive international traveling I saw the vitality of the Church being stimulated by a more open theology than my generic background. News from China, Indonesia and East Africa indicated that God was using "signs and wonders" to build His Church. But I became disillusioned when we were not allowed to air programs of cooperating broadcasters that represented anything other than generic, fundamentalist Christianity. Overseas I knew we had many Pentecostal partners, but the constituency in America was quite conservative, so we catered to them. Meanwhile, I had the joy of meeting some wonderful people like Joseph Tson, Chuck Smith, Alberto Motessi, and some Scandinavian brethren who believed in a more full gospel.

After a brief ministry hiatus while I worked on my doctorate and tried to get a sense of direction for the next step, I became president of a small seminary in Philadelphia. Today I would characterize that era as being reformed, liturgical, evangelical and spiritually sterile as I tried to fit into a sub-culture of the Church that isolated me entirely from anything close to charismatic or Pentecostal theology or experience. Because the seminary was so small, I learned a lot about all aspects of higher education. I also attended and preached at many inner city, minority churches, where experience overrode theology, much to the delight of God, I suspected.

From there we moved west to Colorado Springs, where I assumed the title of director of Higher Education for The Christian and Missionary Alliance. It was very satisfying coming back to my denominational roots organizationally, but about the only part of my job that put me in touch with the heart of Dr. Simpson was giving oversight to the C&MA archives. But it was enough. I hadn't seriously considered our founder since reading his books on the Holy Spirit in order to get ordained nearly two decades earlier. Being part of the "headquarters" team, I realized that the Alliance had a great heritage spurned by some and unknown by most. Through the ministry of Dr. Richard W. Bailey at a leadership retreat, I was called to a proper understanding of the Fourfold Gospel. He helped us see that it is not about salvation, sanctification, healing and the second coming, but about Jesus in these four-fold capacities. This led me to write and preach frequently about *The Centrality of Christ in the Fourfold Gospel*. I knew that I was nearing the heart of Alliance distinctives when I focused on this deeper Christian life.

Warning! Awakening Ahead

In 1993 we moved to Nyack—close to the heart of Alliance history and heritage—to become the eleventh president of Nyack College. I was bringing with me basically the same theology I had been taught there twenty-some years earlier. However, my respect for Alliance missions had grown, and I was open and curious about what made Dr. Simpson tick. I recognized him to be a progressive, nearly radical, visionary in his day, someone who defied labeling, and a man whose spiritual depth and leadership I longed to gain and emulate. The causes he lived for had become dear to me—world evangelization, urban ministry, spiritual renewal, decentralized ecclesiology, Christ-centered theology, and social responsibility. But little did I know when we headed east that it would be a dawning of my spiritual journey.

The Nyack of the 1990's was not what I had known or expected. Chapel services were flat-out wild. Worship was long, loud and lively. When I had been a student, apart from restless chatter during chapel, the decibel level was virtually flat. Now it was super-sonic! At first I was frightened; what would the trustees say if they knew about this? Then I was intimidated. Did these youngsters have something I didn't? Then I was frightened again. Will this split our community, and how do our faculty feel about it anyway?

Gradually, I began to perceive what was happening. Nyack had become ethnically diverse over the past decade, and much of the spiritual energy was coming from African American, Latino, and Asian students. But I noticed most of our (mostly white) Alliance kids joined right in. What's that about, I asked myself. Where's that coming from? The next summer I found out. I attended LIFE, the huge C&MA youth conference held every few years. Worship there was wonderful, almost as good as at Nyack College. I realized that God was doing a new thing in our generation. He was enlivening a radical generation to serve Him radically. And I would be stretched as a sympathizer of the new, radical, relationally rich spirituality that now characterized the new Nyack. Within the next few years I would be renewed, revived and empowered to lead Nyack into an exciting recovery of the "wells" of A. B. Simpson.

Revelation?

A few years later while Betzi and I were visiting friends from the Armonk church who had moved to Brevard, North Carolina, God met me most powerfully one night. Being somewhat of an insomniac, it was not unusual for me to be awake late in the night hours. With no ESPN Sports Center at hand to distract me, I found myself on my face on the floor worshipping the Lord. Suddenly, I was hearing a voice inwardly uttering things that were clearly not within my thought framework. I sensed I was hearing from God, and the "voice" said, "I am giving you the spirit of revelation, wisdom, and discernment." Widely awake, I retorted, almost audibly, "Thank you, but I don't believe in personal revelation." Immediately, I received a gentle rebuke, "What do you think this is, dummy?" Now, I don't know if God would have called me a dummy, but the reply was friendly and humorous in tone.

The revelation went on to inform me about several more things about my ministry as God planned to develop it. For instance, He said I was to "raise up a vanguard of spiritual warriors toward My return." At this point I sensed it was the Lord Jesus talking to me. He gave me some specifics about how to do that and who to do it with. Then He revealed something awful that had happened over thirty years ago in a church I was associated with. This event had led to tragic consequences years later, and the Lord wanted me to reveal it to the existing church leaders. Later, two elders and wives confirmed what the Lord revealed to me, but did not know its causes or effects. Such supernatural revelation was clearly outside my theological comfort zone, and it is not something I actively seek today. But since that night, December 3, 2000, the Lord has revealed new insights and continued to fulfill His words to me.

The effect of that revelation has been a much more dynamic daily walk with God, a more keen awareness of the glorified Christ, and a definite sense of the empowerment of the Holy Spirit in my ministry. I have come to understand revelation as a manifestation of the Holy Spirit that gives evidence of His infilling. And I have come to believe that the too narrow theological box in which I tried to contain God was so very inadequate and unnecessary. I have also come to believe that God wants to manifest Himself very perceptibly to every believer He fills with His Spirit. The manifestations may vary from one individual to another, but the filling of the Holy Spirit is not meant to be taken by faith. God will manifest His presence in an unforgettable way, giving evidence of His deep work.

CHAPTER TWO:
BAPTIZED INTO TRINITARIAN REALITY

At a conference in Florida I was privileged with forty other seminary presidents to sit under the teaching of Dr. Dallas Willard. In five excellent lectures he addressed the topic: *Teaching the Teachers of the Nations.*

Willard stated a beginning proposition this way: "It is God's intent that the ministers of Christ and the people of Christ should be, in him, the light of the world, and should teach all people *what reality is and how to live in it.*" To do this he said we must obey the Great Commission, which he paraphrased this way: "Make disciples of all nations, *submerge them in Trinitarian reality,* and teach them to do all I have commanded you" (my italics), Matt. 28:19-20. During the lecture he used the phrase "…immerse them in Trinitarian community." This requires a "Christian spirituality of a life of obedience to Jesus Christ, training ourselves readily and easily to live out the expectations of Jesus." By *easily,* he did not mean that total obedience to Jesus is easy, but that making the decision of what we intend to do will be easy. We will be so trained in obedience that it becomes natural to obey him.

I was intrigued by this thesis because not only did it provide a new slant on a familiar old text known as the Great Commission, but also because it had the potential to give a fresh understanding to the controversial topic of being baptized in the Holy Spirit. I had never before connected the Spirit-baptism experiences of the early church in Acts with the Great Commission. Nor had I seen Spirit-baptism in relation to the rest of the Trinity. I wondered, is baptism in the Spirit part of the baptizing job of the Great Commission? Have we adequately emphasized the entire Trinity? What did Jesus have in mind by saying, *baptizing them in the name of the Father, Son and Holy Spirit*? Is there a greater affinity than we have perceived between what Jesus was commissioning His followers to do in their discipling ministries and what was happening to the infant church in Jerusalem? Are we short-changing ourselves with an anemic spiritual reality by emphasizing partial Trinitarian baptism?

As I pondered these thoughts I realized that the Trinity is a Unity, and that, while each Person of the Godhead has a specific function to play in creation and in the Church, those who are daughters and sons of the true God have the privilege of walking in right relation to all members of the Trinity. That is why Jesus instructed the disciples to baptize believers into all of the Trinity.

Being immersed in Trinitarian reality needs elaboration. I take it to mean:

- Receiving the Father's forgiveness and love, and walking confidently as his son/daughter
- Being crucified, dead and buried with Christ, risen to a new identity in Him, and living always in worship and obedience to the glorified Jesus Christ
- Being filled daily with the Holy Spirit and growing in spirit-controlled Christ-likeness for holiness and empowerment

Wanting to make sure I was not taking Dr. Willard's thoughts in a direction he did not intend, after I wrote this elaboration on his concept, I sent him a copy, asking for affirmation or clarification. He wrote back and said the ideas fit well within his perspective.

Let us look at each aspect of Trinitarian baptism to expand on the idea.

Baptized in the Reality of the Father's Love

The primary text for unfolding this idea is Matthew 6: 9-13, commonly known as the Lord's Prayer. The first two words seem to be innocent enough, a simple direct address – O*ur Father* – but they reveal two startling truths. The disciples might well have wondered, for whom is Jesus talking when He says *Our*. Whose Father? Jesus'?, the disciples'?, the multitude's?, the Jews'? the Christians'?, all humanity's? Minimally, we would take it to be all those who are followers of Jesus. But even that is radical. Jewish theology did have a concept of God as Father, but the word *Our* suggests a personal dimension that was unheard of, or at least uncommon.

But the more radical notion centers around the word Father – *Abba* – a totally unique form of addressing God, implying an intimacy that most first century Jews would have considered to be bordering on blasphemy. In fact, many pious Jews refused to say the name of God, to avoid taking His name in vain, a prohibition from the Ten Commandments. Nevertheless, God has always wanted an intimate relationship with His people. The word *Father*, referring to God, occurs in several Old Testament passages, notably Isaiah 63:15, 16 and Malachi 1:6. But when Jesus spoke with such intimacy and familiarity about God as *Abba*, it was shocking.

Besides praying to *Abba*, Jesus very definitely taught the idea of God being a personal Father in John 17, where intimacy with the Father is so evident. The Apostle Paul caught the concept, as seen in Galatians 4:6: *And because you are sons, God has sent forth the Spirit of His Son into our hearts, crying, "Abba! Father!"*

Tapping into the father-heart of God is so essential for spiritual intimacy. Best-selling authors like Henri Nouwen, Brennan Manning, Patrick Morley and John Eldredge have been calling our attention to the importance of knowing God intimately as a loving and trustworthy Father. Why do so many people have a jaundiced view of God as Father? In our society of broken families and dysfunctional fatherhood, millions have been spiritually orphaned. Chuck Brewster cites these chilling statistics about American fathering.[10] Young people growing up in fatherless homes account for:

- 63% of youth suicides
- 90% of all homeless and runaway children
- 71% of all high school dropouts
- 80% of rapists motivated with displaced anger
- 85% of all children that exhibit behavior disorders
- 75% of all adolescent patients in chemical abuse centers
- 85% of all youth sitting in prisons

American fathers have not exactly been good role models. No wonder many people do not enjoy intimacy with the heavenly Father.

This is why being soaked in the Father's love is so important today. The Apostle Paul said to the Corinthians, *In Christ Jesus I became your father* (1 Corinthians 4:15). Many people have never had a spiritual father, so for them it is very difficult to know their spiritual identity, but it is not impossible. Finding your identity as a son or daughter of the eternal, infinite, loving Father God is key to having a productive life and ministry. Without Father-baptism, you will not have the confidence you need to achieve your potential. That may be the main message of the Lord's Prayer. No doubt the disciples were intrigued and even amazed by the level of intimacy Jesus assumed as He spoke to and about God. Being saturated in the Father's love is crucial, as the disciples learned.

The basis of that relationship is grace, not effort. All of us are prodigal sons or daughters (see Luke 15:11-32). Some are like the prodigal that squandered his father's inheritance in riotous, rebellious living. In shame we have returned, repented of our sins and subjected ourselves to the Father's loving authority. Others are like the older prodigal son, who did not consider himself to be prodigal. His true spirit was not evident until the younger one received grace. Then the awful spirit of self-righteousness (the spirit of religion) in him was revealed, as in rebellious insolence he said, *Look! For many years I have been serving you, and I have never neglected a commandment of yours.* Interpretation: "I have been trying to earn my inheritance; you owe me." The older brother knew nothing of grace, nor did he even see his own self-righteous heart. Religious people (like the Pharisees and scribes to whom Jesus was comparing the older brother, as seen in Luke 15:2) are sometimes farther from the father than rebellious sons. *God is opposed to the proud, but gives grace to the humble* (James 4:6). Embracing the Father's love and being baptized in His name requires the humility of a repentant sinner.

Moving on into the prayer, we hear Jesus suggest a paradox. After establishing the closest intimacy by directly addressing *Our Father*, Jesus then admonishes the highest reverence: *Hallowed be Thy name*. This part of the prayer demonstrates the inevitable limitation to the intimacy. Well did Jesus know the vastness of God. Well did He know the Father whose presence caused the Israelites to tremble. As appropriate as it was to call God *Father*, it was even more reasonable to encourage the disciples to approach Him with great carefulness and reverence—so much so that He indulged their Jewish scruples by referring to *Thy name*, which means His personhood. The very name of God, into which we are baptized, is to be held in the highest esteem and reverence.

The rest of "the Lord's Prayer" continues this paradox of intimacy and reverence. Notice:

Reverence	Intimacy
Who art in heaven	Our Father
Hallowed be Thy name	
Thy kingdom	come
Thy will be done on earth as it is in heaven	
	Give us this day our daily bread
Forgive us our debts as we also have forgiven our debtors	
Do not lead us into temptation	but deliver us from evil
For Thine is the kingdom, and the power and the glory forever	

The great old hymn *Holy, Holy, Holy* includes the wonderful phrase describing God as "Merciful and Mighty," suggesting this duality of His attributes. Being baptized into the Father qualifies us for receiving His fullness. He is available to meet our deepest needs.

We might ask, what aspect of the Father do we need to be immersed in today? The Lord's Prayer includes all of these.

- His personal intimacy?
- His transcendent reverence?
- His sovereignty as King of the Kingdom?
- His presence?
- His moral will?
- His provision of daily material needs?
- His forgiveness and mercy?
- His protection from the evil one?
- His power?
- His glory?

Jesus invites us to pray for all of these things and expect that the loving Father will provide all this for those who are saturated in the Father.

Baptized in the Reality of the Glorified Jesus

If we are to see the Great Commission fulfilled in our own lives and those we are called to disciple, we will need to be baptized into Jesus, that is, in His name. Much can be said about His incomparable Name and its power, and although *He is the same yesterday, today and forever* (Hebrews 13:8), we need to know Him as He is now.

In Scripture we meet Jesus in four different manifestations.
- In the Old Testament He appears in Christophanies
- In the New Testament He first appears as Jesus of Nazareth
- For forty days He was the Resurrected Jesus
- **In the Revelation He is the Glorified Jesus**

Jesus spoke about His pre-existence in John 8:58, saying, ...*before Abraham was born, I am.* An example of His appearing is in Daniel 3:25, where He was the fourth man in the fire. We do not know Him this way.

Most of us first meet Him as Jesus of Nazareth. We acquire and often maintain sort of a Sunday School knowledge of Jesus. For many people He is just Baby Jesus, Boy Jesus, Rabbi, Messiah, or Crucifix. But this is not how He appears today.

For forty days He was the Resurrected Jesus. This was a mysterious existence. On the one hand, He had a material body; He ate bread and fish. On the other hand, He had a spiritual body; for example, He walked through a door. During this time He was recognized and seen by more than five hundred people. But this is not how He appears now, nor will we know Him this way.

Now He is the Glorified Jesus. This is the Jesus we must get to know and into whom we must be baptized. He is described in a book specifically written to reveal Him to us, *The Revelation of Jesus Christ.* The descriptions are written in apocalyptic language in passages such as Revelation 1:12-16:

I saw one like the Son of Man, clothed with a long robe and with a golden sash across his chest. His head and his hair were white as white wool, white as snow; his eyes were like a flame of fire, his feet were like burnished bronze, refined as in a furnace, and his voice was like the sound of many waters. In his right hand he held seven stars, and from his mouth came a sharp, two-edged sword, and his face was like the sun shining with full force.

And Revelation 19:11-16:

Then I saw heaven opened, and there was a white horse! Its rider is called Faithful and True, and in righteousness he judges and makes war. His eyes are like a flame of fire, and on his head are many diadems; and he has a name inscribed that no one knows but himself. He is clothed in a robe dipped in blood, and his name is called The Word of God. And the armies of heaven, wearing fine linen, white and pure, were following him on white horses. From his mouth comes a sharp sword with which to strike down the nations, and he will rule them with a rod of iron; he will tread the wine press of the fury of the wrath of God the Almighty. On his robe and on his thigh he has a name inscribed, "King of kings and Lord of lords." (Both passages quoted from the NRSV.)

What the images suggest is that He is now enthroned with the Father, and appears as a conquering warrior, soon to return to His people in total victory. The meeting will be a loving union of Bridegroom and bride.

Many believers in Jesus—even ones who have walked with Christ for years—relate only to the Jesus of yesterday, and have not yet encountered the Glorified Jesus. Maybe it's because we do not read Revelation or understand its strange images, or we read it as the revelation of the future, not the revelation of Jesus Christ.

Fruitful Abiding

Being baptized into Jesus brings us into complete union with Him. Romans 6:4-5 describes this union.

Therefore we have been buried with Him through baptism into death, in order that as Christ was raised from the dead through the glory of the Father, so we too might walk in newness of life. For if we have become united with Him in the likeness of His death, certainly we shall be also in the likeness of His resurrection...

Jesus used a similar idea to describe this union. Looking ahead to the time of His glorified existence, Jesus invited His disciples into an ongoing intimate relationship with Him. In John 15 He used the imagery of a vine and its branches. Some branches, He said, bear no fruit, so they are taken away (verse 2), gathered and burned (verse 6). Other branches bear some fruit; these are pruned, or cut back to eliminate unnecessary parts so they can be more fruitful. Other branches bear much fruit. They are very productive because they stay connected to the vine (verse 5) and use all of their resources to allow the nourishing sap of the vine to flow through them and produce the fruit. As the vine, Jesus continues to give fruitful life to the branches that stay connected to Him.

Analysis of the context of this teaching shows a progression in this relationship:
1. As His disciples we will bear much fruit (verse 8)
2. To Bear Fruit we must Abide (verses 4, 5)
3. To Abide we must Obey (verse 10)
4. To Obey we must Love (verses 14:23, 24)
5. To Love we must Know Him (verse 15)

But, of course to really know Him we must abide in Him.

What kind of fruit will the branches bear when they remain connected to the vine? Some Bible students believe Jesus was talking about the fruit of soul winning or disciple-making. Perhaps so. Maybe He meant the kind of fruit that Paul called the fruit of the Spirit. I believe this is a more likely interpretation because in John 14 Jesus had just been telling them what the role of the Holy Spirit would be in their lives.

The nine qualities that Paul mentioned in Galatians 5 are all seen in other passages to be the kind of Christ-like virtues that will mature in us. As we abide in Jesus we will produce:

- **Love**: John 15:12 - *This is my commandment, that you love one another, just as I have loved you.*
- **Joy**: John 15:11 – *These things have I spoken to you, that My joy may be in you, and that your joy may be made full.*
- **Peace**: John 14:27 – *Peace I leave with you; My peace I give to you.*
- **Patience**: Ephesians 4:2 – *Walk worthy of your calling with patience, showing forbearance...*
- **Kindness**: Ephesians 4:32 – *Be kind to one another.*

- **Goodness**: Galatians 6:10 – *Do good to all men, especially to those who are of the household of faith.*
- **Faithfulness**: Proverbs 12:22 – *Those who deal faithfully are God's delight.*
- **Gentleness**: 1 Timothy 6:11 – *Pursue after...gentleness.*
- **Self-control**: 2 Peter 1:6 – *Add to your knowledge self-control.*

The results of bearing much fruit, or staying connected to the Glorified Jesus, are:
- Answered prayers (verse 7)
- God is glorified (verse 8)
- We are truly disciples of Christ (verse 8)
- Full joy (11)
- We are friends of Jesus (15)

This kind of intimate relationship with the Glorified Jesus Christ is possible only if we are truly saturated in Him. Other biblical terminology that suggests this relationship includes: Dying to Self (Luke 9:23) and Baptized into Union with Him (Romans 6:1-5). But the key to being fruitful, effective disciples of Jesus is to find our full identity in Him. When we are baptized in His name, we take on that new identity. The Glorified Jesus invites us to be immersed in His reality by abiding in Him.

Buried Alive

Perhaps this is a good time to reflect on how the actual ordinance or sacrament of water baptism, relates to its metaphorical use that I have suggested was in Jesus' mind when He gave the Great Commission. A good starting point is to consider the baptism of Jesus because I believe that that strange event gives insight into the heart of Jesus and His understanding of the significance of baptism.

The Gospel of Matthew simply states that Jesus came from Galilee to the Jordan to be baptized by John. Recognizing Jesus as the "Coming One" (Messiah), John was reluctant to baptize Him. However, Jesus insisted on being baptized by John, saying that *it is proper for us to do this to fulfill all righteousness* (Matthew 3:15).

The baptism of Jesus confounds many theologians. If John's baptism was, as he said, a baptism for the repentance and remission of sin, why would Jesus who was sinless ask to be baptized? Would not onlookers assume that Jesus was confessing sins and the need for cleansing? Why would He join the ranks of other sinners and submit to this rather unorthodox ritual? Two ideas may help us.

First, notice that immediately after Jesus was baptized, heaven was opened and the Spirit of God descended like a dove upon Jesus, and an audible voice from heaven said, "This is my Son whom I love. With him I am well pleased." We assume that this heavenly message was given audibly for the benefit of the listening crowd. Could it be, however, that the message was also for Jesus?

Might it be that this was really the first temptation of Jesus? Would He be humble enough to identify with sinners by going into the water of baptism? Perhaps that's what Jesus meant when He said, "it is proper for us to do this to fulfill all righteousness." By humbling Himself, Jesus demonstrated the route He would choose in His ministry—namely, identifying with sinners—and thus the Father exonerated Him and reaffirmed that relationship by commending Jesus with the words, "This is my Son whom I love. With him I am well pleased."

Clearly, the water and Spirit baptism of Jesus was a defining moment in His earthly life. After *the Holy Spirit descended upon Him in bodily form like a dove* (Luke 3:22), His public ministry began. Submitting to baptism was a powerful way to identify with humanity fully. Though He was the Son of God in His pre-incarnate existence, and even before His baptism, from that time on He more fully entered into the messianic part of His life—*messiah*, meaning "anointed one." And so during His earthy life Jesus ministered powerfully through the anointing of the Holy Spirit that was on Him. Peter referred to this when he was ministering to the Gentiles with Cornelius in Caesarea:

> *...you yourselves know the thing which took place throughout all Judea, starting from Galilee, after the baptism which John proclaimed. You know of Jesus of Nazareth, how God anointed Him with the Holy Spirit and with power, and how He went about doing good, and healing all who were oppressed by the devil; for God was with Him* (Acts 10:37, 38).

During those thirty-three years, Jesus
> *...was truly the eternal God, very God, of very God. But when He came down from yonder heights of glory He suspended the direct operation of His own independent power and became voluntarily dependent on the power of God through the Holy Ghost.... He purposely took His place side by side with us, heeding equally with the humblest disciple the constant power of God to sustain Him in all His work.... And so He went through life in the position of dependence, that He might be our public example and teach us that we too have the same secret of strength and power that He possessed, and that as surely as He overcame through the Holy Ghost, so may we.*[11]

Second, we must realize that John represented something quite new in Judaism. It is not exaggerating to say that he initiated a renewal movement within Jewish religion. His ministry separated the staid and proud Jews, who saw no need to repent, from those who recognized that their family lineage and nationality were not enough to give them an authentic relationship with God.

In reality, John brought about a first century reformation. Whereas the traditional religious faith seemed to depend on external conditions—namely, Jewishness, circumcision, and adherence to the law—John came preaching a message of inner transformation beginning with repentance.

Later in His ministry, Jesus used John as a decisive dividing line within Judaism. Being insidiously tested by enemies who wanted to trap Jesus into heresy, Jesus asked, "John's baptism – was it from heaven, or from men? Answer me!" (Mark 11:30). Jesus insisted that they take a stand on what was a critical issue. Of course they chose not to take such a stand because it would not have been popular to speak against John. Yet they surely did not want to identify with John's movement.

I'm suggesting here that one reason Jesus submitted to the baptism of John was to declare to the Jewish nation that He readily identified with the Jewish renewal movement which was occurring. He affirmed John's message of the need to repent, humbly submitted to baptism, and by example He led the way into those waters for millions of Christians who subsequently would repent and humbly be buried with Jesus in baptism. And it might well be argued that this radical act also reveals to us the thinking about Jesus vis a vis the importance of renewal in the midst of stale religion.

Baptism, like any other spiritual activity, can be conducted merely as an external ritual without sincerity and reverence. It is possible in baptism to come out different in only one way—wetter—but wetter is not necessarily better. So what should we think about our baptism? With regard to Jesus, it is a covenant, a determination to live wholeheartedly for Christ. Just as He was willing to identify with sinners, so do we fully identify with Him in the burial waters. With regard to ourselves, it is a turning point, in our transformation into the character of Christ. With regard to the Church, it is a visual, public testimony that we have received Christ into our life, and others can expect to see us living for Him. With regard to the world, we should consider baptism as our "coming out party," the time when we say to the world that we will no longer live by its values but have changed our citizenship to the kingdom of God. Baptism should never be a private affair; it is always a public statement that we are new persons in Christ and have set our course to follow him.

Can water baptism and Spirit baptism be simultaneous? It surely can, and probably should be the norm rather than the exception. One person who interacted with me on this book offered this testimony:

For me personally, physical baptism and baptism in the Spirit were simultaneous and led to a richer, deeper insight of being filled throughout my whole being with the Spirit and a deeper understanding of Christ Himself and the Spirit's role in revealing Christ to me. In other words, I "knew" in my mind and heart because the word of testimony that God's Spirit gave through me at the point of baptism came out of my heart and mouth to others. The whole beautiful story of "Christ in you, the hope of glory" and "being filled with the Spirit" I suddenly saw, knew, understood, felt, desired completely, and yet with a sense of even more richness and deeper understanding still available. This is my testimony and not that of others, nor are physical baptism and Spirit baptism necessarily simultaneous, of course. And I doubt that these words are capturing my own experience adequately. My point is that the beginning of the story is the experience itself, and while it has manifestations, it also had knowledge and understanding like never before and leads to a life lived in Christ, a work of the Spirit in us.

I suspect that if full teaching about water baptism and Spirit baptism were more often given, many more people would receive them simultaneously. This should surely be a concern of pastors today.

Baptized in the Reality of the Holy Spirit

What we are really talking about here is a phrase that used to scare me greatly: being baptized in the Holy Spirit. What does this phrase mean?

First, let's look at some of the ways Jesus said the Holy Spirit would relate to His followers. These are benefits of being baptized or immersed in the reality of the Holy Spirit:

- John 14:16 – The Spirit will remain with you forever
- John 14:17 – He is the Spirit of truth; He is with you and will be in you
- John 14:26 – As the Helper, He will teach you and remind you all that Jesus said
- John 15:26 – He comes from the Father and bears witness of Jesus

- John 16:8 – He convicts the world of sin, righteousness and judgment
- John 16:13 – He will guide you into all truth and disclose what is to come
- John 16:14 – He will glorify Jesus

These great blessings that come from our relationship with the Holy Spirit should not threaten us, but give us great confidence and assurance that the Father and the Son will continue to work in us and through us through the agency of the third Person of the Godhead. The Greek term used frequently to describe Him is *Paracletos*, which means Comforter or Encourager. So it is quite ironic that the very agent meant to bring comfort and encouragement has become in the Church a source of controversy and division. We will unpack reasons for this strange development as we go along, but for now, we must realize that as surely as God wants us to be baptized into the Father and Son, so does He also want us to be baptized into the Holy Spirit.

In the next chapter we examine the relationship between being baptized in the Holy Spirit and being filled with the Holy Spirit. We should note here, however, that experiences with the Holy Spirit did not begin at Pentecost. Scripture shows that both pre-Christian Old and New Testament people were empowered for moments of specific activities or insights. Bezalel, for example, was one of the skilled craftsmen assigned by Moses to work on the tabernacle. In Exodus 31:3 God tells Moses, *I have filled him with the Spirit of God in wisdom, in understanding, in knowledge, and in all kinds of craftsmanship...*

Samson, the strong man antihero during the period of the Judges, was capable of super-human deeds of strength because *the Spirit of the Lord came upon him mightily* (Judges 14:6, 19; 15:14). After his sin against Uriah and Bathsheba, David prayed in Psalm 51:11 that God would *take not Thy Holy Spirit from me.* Isaiah reports about the Israelites in Isaiah 63:10, 11

But they rebelled
And grieved His Holy Spirit;

> *Therefore, He turned Himself to become their enemy,*
> *He fought against them.*
>
> *Then His people remembered the days of old, of Moses.*
> *Where is He who brought them up out of the sea with the shepherds*
> *of His flock?*
> *Where is He who **put His Holy Spirit within them**...?*

In the Synoptic Gospels (Matthew, Mark and Luke) we see pre-Pentecost examples of the Holy Spirit's activity. In Matthew 3:11 John (the baptizer) declares that Jesus *will **baptize you with the Holy Spirit** and fire* (parallels in Mark 1:8, Luke 3:16, and John 1:33). Jesus told the Pharisees in Matthew 12:28 that he would **cast out demons by the Spirit of God.** In Matthew 22:43 Jesus implied that David spoke (or wrote) by the Holy Spirit: "**How does David in the Spirit call Him Lord?**" (parallel in Mark 12:36).

In Luke 1:15 the angel said regarding John (the baptizer), ... **he will be filled with the Holy Spirit while yet in his mother's womb.** But John wasn't the only one in the family who would know the activity of the Spirit. In 1:41 Luke writes, **... and Elizabeth was filled with the Holy Spirit and cried out with a loud voice,** and in 1:67, **...his father Zacharias was filled with the Holy Spirit and prophesied....**

Regarding Simeon, in 2:25 Luke reports, the **Holy Spirit was upon him. It had been revealed to him....** Then we read about Jesus in 4:1, **Jesus, full of the Holy Spirit, returned from the Jordan and was led....** Later in 10:21 [Jesus] **rejoiced greatly in the Holy Spirit, and said, "I praise You, O Father...."**

From these verses we see that the events leading up to the incarnation of Jesus were sovereignly orchestrated by God and demanded the full involvement of the Holy Spirit. We also see that Jesus was very conscious as an adult that the Spirit was upon Him, leading Him and inspiring His ministry.

John's Gospel gives more theological insight into what the disciples could expect as they encountered the Spirit's fullness. Jesus spoke to Nicodemus in John 3:5 about being *born of water and the Spirit.* Later in the same chapter John refers to Jesus by saying in 3:34, *He gives the Spirit without measure.* In John 7:39 Jesus *spoke of the Spirit, whom those who believed in Him were to receive, for the Spirit was not yet (given) because Jesus was not yet glorified.*

John 14-17 gives some of the richest teaching in Scripture about the Holy Spirit, but we will note just one idea, that found in 14:16, 17: *He will give you another "Helper" that He may be with you forever; that is the Spirit of truth...He abides with you and will be in you.* Then when He came to the disciples after His resurrection John reports that, *He breathed on them and said to them, "Receive the Holy Spirit"* (20:22).

The Apostle John recalled from the teachings and ministry of Jesus that believers would be born of the Holy Spirit and would receive the Spirit fully after Jesus was glorified (in heaven). The Spirit would be a permanent Presence in the believers.

Pre-Pentecostal Preaching

Up to this point, no doubt the concept of the Holy Spirit was merely a theological notion to the disciples. They were certainly aware that there was something unique about Jesus and had perhaps witnessed His baptism when the Holy Spirit descended upon Him as a dove. But they were still unempowered spectators in the work of the kingdom of God.

In many believers today, even though the Holy Spirit has been poured out and is present and active in the world and the Church, there is little evidence of Spirit empowerment. While it is true that everyone who is born again is born of the Spirit and has the Spirit resident within, many Christians have not experienced the baptism and filling of the Holy Spirit.

Some are just not aware of this blessing, as was true of the Ephesian believers in Acts 19, who were converted to Christ under the ministry of Apollos, a brilliant man with impeccable credentials – *learned, with a thorough knowledge of the Scriptures ... instructed in the ways of the Lord.* His preaching was compelling as he *spoke with great fervor and taught about Jesus accurately....* And he was bold. Visiting the synagogues to confront his Jewish kinsmen with the claims of the resurrected Jesus, *he vigorously refuted the Jews in public debate, proving from the Scriptures that Jesus was the Christ* (Acts 18:24-28).

What bishop or superintendent wouldn't be thrilled to have a young, intellectual evangelist and apologete like this in his district? Apollos even had a pastoral bearing, being *a great help to those who by grace had believed.* Furthermore, he was a cosmopolitan man, quite comfortable in mixing in diverse settings, having been raised in Alexandria (northern Africa). The Church seemed quite comfortable sending Apollos on itinerant ministries. We first meet him in Corinth, after his very successful evangelistic campaign in Ephesus. Blessing just seemed to follow him around.

But Apollos' preaching and teaching were pre-pentecostal. Acts 19 tells about Paul visiting the Ephesians after Apollos' campaign, only to find out that the believers there didn't know anything about the Holy Spirit. The disciples Paul found in Ephesus were like their spiritual father Apollos – fervent in spirit, but not filled with the Spirit.

Like Apollos, the ministry of many evangelicals is devoid of the Holy Spirit's fire. Getting by with good training and excellent academic preparation, they delight in imparting information. But for some reason, few who listen are empowered for spiritual warfare, like the Ephesians would soon face in Acts 19. Fortunately, Apollos was quick to learn and to receive the Spirit's fullness, submitting humbly to the teaching of Priscilla and Aquila. And fortunately, Paul followed up the campaign in Ephesus and laid his hands upon the believers who were then filled with the Holy Spirit.

For nearly a half century I have been listening to preaching and teaching in evangelical churches, and most of what I have heard has been pre-pentecostal Apollos preaching. Rarely have I heard challenges about being filled with the Holy Spirit, and almost never have I heard preachers invite people for prayer to receive an impartation of the Holy Spirit. Whatever happened to Pentecost? Have we been so frightened by what we consider to be excesses that we have sent the Holy Spirit back to Jesus as an unwanted gift? No, the Spirit is still here on planet Earth; in the eastern and southern hemispheres, where the Church is growing seven times faster than in North America, the Holy Spirit is active and dynamic. Many of the poorest countries economically are the richest spiritually.

This is a plea for evangelical leaders throughout the West to get over their pneumaphobia, to quit worrying about their reputation and the labels people may pin on them, and to receive a fresh baptism of Holy Spirit anointing so they can preach and impart the Holy Spirit to the disciples of Apollos who fill our churches.

I believe that there are many evangelical Christians who are aware of the baptism and filling of the Holy Spirit, but have not had the opportunity to receive a ministry of impartation. Still others adamantly resist this part of the Christian life because they fear the excesses they have seen in some who claim to be Spirit-filled and project themselves as spiritually superior.

In succeeding chapters I hope to demonstrate that Spirit-filled Christian living does not lead to eccentricity, weirdness or arrogance. On the contrary, Spirit-filled living, initiated by the baptism of the Holy Spirit and perpetuated by multiple fillings, is the "normal Christian life," and is required for a victorious and effective spiritual life.

CHAPTER THREE:
THE ACTS OF THE HOLY SPIRIT

Jesus said that when the Spirit would come, the Holy Spirit's greatest ministry in the Church would be glorifying Jesus Christ, the Son of God, rather than calling attention to Himself as the third person of the Godhead. After His resurrection, Jesus *breathed on them and said to them, "Receive the Holy Spirit"* (John 20:22). He also said to the disciples, *I am sending forth the promise of My Father upon you; but you are to stay in the city until you are clothed with power from on high* (Luke 24:49). In Acts 1:8 He told them that the power who would come upon them is the Holy Spirit. If we are to have such an all-encompassing relationship with the Holy Spirit, we would be wise to know as much about Him as possible.

Perhaps because the Holy Spirit may not seem quite as personal to us as our Father in heaven or as Jesus, the Son, it is easy for us to think of him as third in importance. Pastor David Pawson in England referred to this lack of emphasis on the Holy Spirit in this humorous over-generalization: The Catholics believe in "God the Father, God the Son, and God the Holy Virgin" and the Protestants believe in "God the Father, God the Son, and God the Holy Scriptures." Where is the Holy Spirit?

In the Old Testament we are confronted with God the Father, who was very personal to the Jews. He led and judged them, provided their needs, and spoke directly to them through the prophets.

In the New Testament we meet the second person of the Godhead, Jesus Christ, the personal, incarnate expression of God—God in the flesh. We hear His teachings, we see Him doing many miraculous deeds, we know who His friends were, and we know relatively much about His life.

When it comes to the Holy Spirit, we are not given as much personal information as we might like. Perhaps this is part of God's plan. Without knowing about the Holy Spirit, though, we cannot really say that we know God, for the Holy Spirit is God!

As we saw in the previous chapter, prior to the days of Jesus the Holy Spirit only visited the people of God, coming upon them for special events and activities. One time at a feast Jesus said, *If a man is thirsty, let him come to me and drink. Whoever believes in me, as the Scripture has said, streams of living water will flow from within him* (John 7:37-38). Then John, the Gospel writer, adds this comment in verse 39, *By this he meant the Spirit, whom those who believed in him were later to receive. Up to that time the Spirit had not been given, since Jesus had not yet been glorified.* We learn from this verse that the Spirit of God would be given to the people of God when Jesus would be glorified, that is when He ascended into heaven after His resurrection and assumed His rightful place with God the Father. We also learn that the Holy Spirit would be given to those who believe in Jesus. They were later to receive the Holy Spirit as Jesus had promised.

The Holy Spirit dwells in the lives of people who know Jesus personally. Jesus told Nicodemus that unless a man is born again, he cannot enter the kingdom of God (John 3:5). Paul taught in Romans, *And if anyone does not have the Spirit of Christ, he does not belong to Christ* (Romans 8:9). If you know Jesus Christ personally through faith, then the Holy Spirit lives within you. This is not to say that you have gone as far as you might go in your relationship with the Holy Spirit or that you have been filled with the Spirit, but you can be sure of the fact that if you are a born-again Christian, the Holy Spirit lives within you.

Spirit At Work

The work of the Holy Spirit is normally accomplished in and through Christian believers, as they are available to be used by Him. The Scriptures list at least eighteen tasks routinely fulfilled by the Holy Spirit:

1. Convicts of the sin of unbelief (John 16:8)
2. Convinces that Jesus is the righteousness of God (John 16:10)
3. Convinces that the power of Satan has been broken (John 16:11)
4. Reveals God's Word (Acts 1:16; 28:25; 2 Timothy 3:16)
5. Guides into all truth (John 16:13)
6. Comforts (John 14:16-26)
7. Glorifies Jesus Christ (John 16:14)
8. Regenerates (John 3:3, 5)
9. Indwells (Romans 8:11)
10. Gives joy (Romans 14:17)
11. Anoints (1 John 2:20, 27)
12. Sanctifies (Romans 15:16; 2 Thessalonians 2:13)
13. Gives discernment (1 Corinthians 2:10-16; 1 John 4:1-6)
14. Seals (Ephesians 1:13)
15. Baptizes (Acts 2:17-41)
16. Infills (Acts 2:4)
17. Empowers (Micah 3:8)
18. Distributes spiritual gifts (1 Corinthians 12:3-11)

Clearly the pouring out or baptizing of the Holy Spirit that took place at Pentecost was a unique event. Other great blessings of the Spirit's visitation have occurred in revivals, but the initial outpouring of the Spirit on the Church, as promised by Jesus, was truly a "one-off" event. What is immediately evident from the account in Acts 2 is that the disciples were radically changed. They who had been cowering in fear became recklessly bold in their witness. What had changed? The resurrection of Jesus? That was not it. He had been with them for forty days after His resurrection, but they were not yet changed. Their theology was correct, but they still lacked spiritual power.

What changed was their entire spiritual circuitry. At Pentecost they were totally rewired by the Holy Spirit. So different were they that those who saw and heard them thought they were drunk (Acts 2:15). They were filled, inebriated, saturated, immersed, baptized in and with the Holy Spirit.

Some say that since that event was unique we are not to look for or expect any further such manifestations. However, the promise was not just to the fathers but also to the children. Pentecost will never happen again as it did in the upper room, but there is a personal Pentecostal experience available for every believer. And those who never welcome it will not be filled with the Spirit or enabled to abide in Christ as fruit-bearing believers.

While the idea of being baptized in the Holy Spirit is threatening to some believers and celebrated by others, what many do not know is that this experience relates to other spiritual experiences like being filled with the Holy Spirit. Can a person be a Christian without being baptized in water? Yes, but not an obedient Christian. Can a person be a Christian without being baptized in the Holy Spirit? Yes, but not an empowered Christian. Spirit baptism is not a luxury reserved for the spiritually elite. It is a blessing the Lord wants for all His people.

Born, Baptized, and Filled

What are we to expect in our personal Pentecostal experience? What is it like to be baptized in the Holy Spirit? At this point it will be useful to describe the relationship between being baptized in the Holy Spirit and being filled with the Holy Spirit.

There are many Bible scholars who believe that Spirit-baptism is the same as conversion. They argue that the Holy Spirit comes into us as soon as we are born of the Spirit. In fact, they may point to John 3 where Jesus told Nicodemus that to be born again is to be born of the

Spirit. But is being born of the Spirit the same as being baptized in the Spirit? If so, what was the condition of the disciples pre-Pentecost? Were they not yet saved? Had one of them died before the Pentecostal event, would he not have gone to be with Jesus? It seems to me that Spirit-baptism is usually a definite act subsequent to salvation. I say "usually" because usually in our day we do not teach or minister the filling of the Holy Spirit at the time of conversion or soon after. But in the early church it was not so. Notice the instructions Jesus gave to Ananias as He commissioned him to minister to Paul.

> *"Brother Saul, the Lord – Jesus, who appeared to you on the road as you were coming here – has sent me so that you may see again and be filled with the Holy Spirit." Immediately, something like scales fell from Saul's eyes, and he could see again. He got up and was baptized…(Acts 9:17, 18).*

Notice two ideas: Jesus was eager for Paul to be filled with the Holy Spirit immediately after his conversion, and Paul was filled with the Holy Spirit before he was water baptized. From this, maybe we should infer that water baptism is meant to be the outward symbol of the inward reality of being Spirit-baptized.

The Greek word *baptizo* means saturated or immersed. Think of a sponge. If it is immersed in water, it becomes saturated, and is filled. A believer's first filling with the Holy Spirit is, I believe, his or her baptism in the Holy Spirit. It occurs only once, whereas fillings will occur often. The baptism in the Holy Spirit will likely be a dramatic event, or at least have dramatic after-effects. These effects are called *manifestations of the Spirit*, and they provide evidence of His filling, which gives us the spiritual confidence we need to serve God effectively.

What are Manifestations?

Often when spiritual gifts are discussed, the manifestations are lumped together with the gifts. I believe Paul made a clear distinction as he wrote to the Corinthians, and unpacking that distinction is at the heart of this book and our understanding of how we can learn to walk in our anointing.

Manifestations are observable evidences of God's presence which He gives so that every person who is filled with the Holy Spirit will have the assurance of that initial filling or baptism. The manifestations in 1 Corinthians 12 are spiritual experiences that give that evidence – things like a word of wisdom and a gift of healing. But before going more deeply into this concept, let us examine other usages of the Greek word for manifestation, *phanerosis*.

The primary meaning of *phanerosis* is <u>manifestation</u>, which is the translation used in a key verse we will be exploring further, 1 Corinthians 12:7 – *But to each one is given the manifestation of the Spirit for the common good.*

A common translation is simply to <u>make or become known</u>, found in:
- Matthew 12:16 (Jesus warned the people he healed not to <u>make Him known</u>)
- Mark 3:12 (Jesus warned the demons not to <u>make Him known</u>)
- Mark 6:14 (His name had <u>become well known)</u>
- Philippians 1:13 (Christ has <u>become well known</u>)

Mark 4:22 and parallel passage Luke 8:17 use the word twice where it means to <u>be revealed</u> or <u>come to light</u>, referring to the light of a lamp.

In several cases *phanerosis* refers to something being or becoming evident
- 1 Timothy 4:15 – Timothy's progress should <u>become evident</u> to all
- Romans 1:19 – that which is known about God <u>is evident</u> within them
- 1 Corinthians 3:13 – each man's work will <u>become evident</u>
- 1 Corinthians 11:19 – those who are approved may have <u>become evident</u>
- Galatians 5:19 – the deeds of the flesh <u>are evident</u>

Other uses of the word include

- Acts 4:16 – the fact that a noteworthy miracle has taken place through them <u>is apparent</u> to all
- Romans 2:28 – nor is circumcision <u>outward</u>
- 1 Corinthians 14:25 – the secrets of his heart are <u>disclosed</u>
- 2 Corinthians 4:2 – the <u>manifestation</u> of truth

From all of the references to gifts in relation to the Holy Spirit we learn that the Holy Spirit is the Gift (*dorea*); He dispenses individualized gifts *(charismata)* as He chooses, which manifest outwardly or make apparent (*phanerosis*) the reality of God.

When we are baptized in or with the Holy Spirit, we can expect God to manifest Himself as evidence of His presence and fullness, which will empower our spiritual gift in ministries He chooses for us to bring glory to Jesus Christ. Being immersed in Trinitarian reality means nothing less than this.

Manifestations in Acts

In the Acts of the Apostles, which some have said should be entitled "The Acts of the Holy Spirit," we see the dynamic of Spirit baptism and filling on many occasions, which I have indicated below with **bold print,** and we see accompanying manifestations, or evidences of the Spirit's activity, which I have **<u>underlined</u>**. In some cases the manifestation is implied, which I have supplied in parentheses. All of these references are in the book of Acts.

In 1:5 Jesus told the disciples, *You will be **baptized with the Holy Spirit** not many days from now,* and in 1:8. *You will **receive power** when the Holy Spirit has come upon you.* Then in 2:4, *they were all **filled with the Holy Spirit and <u>began to speak with other tongues</u>** as the Spirit was giving them utterance.*

At the end of his sermon on the day of Pentecost, after calling the people to repentance, Peter in 2:38 said, … *you will receive the gift of the Holy Spirit.* Then in 4:8, *Peter, **filled with the Holy Spirit,** said to them…* **(boldness, prophecy)**, and he told them that it was in the name of Jesus

45

that he had healed the lame man. Later, the believers were together celebrating the power of their witness, *And when they had prayed, the place where they had been gathered together was shaken and **they were all filled with the Holy Spirit and <u>began to speak the Word of God with boldness</u>*** (4:31).

When the church needed to expand its leadership base, they chose *seven men of good reputation and **full of the Spirit and of <u>wisdom</u>*** (6:3). One of them was *Stephen, a man **<u>full of faith</u> and the Holy Spirit*** (6:3). Later while Stephen was being stoned because of his witness, ***being full of the Holy Spirit,** he gazed intently into heaven and saw the glory of God and Jesus* **(revelation).**

In 8:14-17 Peter and John went to the Samaritans *that they might receive the Holy Spirit for He had not yet fallen upon any of them… they had simply been baptized in the name of the Lord Jesus…they began laying their hands on them and **they were receiving the Holy Spirit**.* Something visible must have happened because it was evident to Simon the magician, who tried to buy the power.

In 9:17-20 Ananias was sent to Saul *that you may regain your sight and be filled with the Holy Spirit, <u>and **immediately he regained his sight (healing)**</u>, got up and was baptized…and **<u>began to proclaim Jesus in the synagogues.</u>***

Thus far, Jews, Proselytes and Samaritans have received the Holy Spirit. In chapter 10, the Lord instructs Peter to go minister to Cornelius, the first Gentile convert. In 10:44, *While Peter was still speaking, the Holy Spirit fell upon all those who were listening. All were amazed because the gift of the Holy Spirit had been poured out on the Gentiles also, for they were hearing them **<u>speaking with tongues and exalting God</u>…(they) received the Holy Spirit just as we did**.* Later, explaining the situation to the other apostles and brethren in Jerusalem, Peter said, *the Holy Spirit fell upon them **just as He did upon us** at the beginning. And I remembered the word of the Lord, how he used to say "John baptized with water, but you will be baptized with the Holy Spirit"* (11:15).

In 11:24 Barnabas is described as *a good man and full of the Holy Spirit and of faith.* Near the beginning of his first missionary journey, Paul encountered Elymas the magician who was trying to undermine the ministry to the proconsul, so in 13:9, *Paul, filled with the Holy Spirit, fixed his gaze on him and said...* **(binding).** Later in 13:52, *the disciples were continually filled with joy and the Holy Spirit.*

An insightful passage about the relationship between conversion and the receiving of the Holy Spirit is found in chapter 19, where in verse 2 Paul asked some Ephesian disciples of John the Baptist, *Did you receive the Holy Spirit when you believed?* After they admitted that they hadn't even heard of the Holy Spirit, in 19:6, *When Paul laid his hands on them, the Holy Spirit came upon them, and they began speaking with tongues and prophesying.* This occurred immediately after their conversion to Christ and water baptism.

These passages from Acts suggest that whenever the Holy Spirit baptizes a person or group, at least one of the manifestations of the Spirit will be evident. Or to say it another way, when the Spirit comes in fullness, something happens that manifests God's presence and activity. In Acts it is clear that people never had to "take it by faith" that the Holy Spirit was present and active. There was always some dynamic evidence, which Paul called *manifestations of the Spirit* in 1 Corinthians 12:8. (Most of the underlined words above are manifestations of the Spirit from Paul's list, which we will discuss in chapter five.)

Spiritual Inferiority Complexes

Imagine walking with Jesus literally for three years. You hear His very profound, courageous and authoritative teaching; you see His amazing healings, miracles over nature, and expelling of demons; and you receive His frequent admonitions of your lack of faith because you cannot do the things He does. All this adds up to one colossal spiritual inferiority complex.

And at different times in very difficult circumstances, like when Peter began sinking after walking on the water, you hear Him say, *O you of little faith, why did you doubt?* (Matthew 14:31). When the other nine disciples who did not go with Jesus to the Mount of Transfiguration failed to exorcise a demon from a little boy, Jesus said, *O unbelieving generation, how long shall I be with you? How long shall I put up with you?* (Mark 9:19). And after the disciples awakened Jesus in the boat in the midst of a storm and He stilled the winds and calmed the waves, He said, *Where is your faith?* (Luke 8:25).

Why was Jesus so tough on His disciples? Why did He expect them to do what He as the Son of God could do? Why did He say that after He left them, they would do even greater works than He did (John 14:12)? Might He have known something they did not know? Of course He did. He knew He would be sending the "the Helper," the Holy Spirit (John 15:26), who would empower them to bear witness faithfully and courageously.

Wouldn't you agree that we are so much like the first disciples before Pentecost? So often we want to walk in spiritual power and rise above our natural abilities, but for some reason, we live a rather predictable, uninspired life. We read about the great exploits of other believers, or we hear amazing, powerful sermons, or we may even be present when someone is healed, but our own spiritual confidence is low. We hesitate to step out of the natural order of life to call upon God to intervene with the divine order. We just lack confidence. And we may feel guilty because we know we are to be like Jesus. In Luke 6:40, Jesus said, *A disciple is not above the teacher, but everyone who is fully qualified will be like the teacher.* But we don't feel very much like Jesus.

Of course, maybe what Jesus meant was that we will become like Him in character, not empowerment. But even here we have a problem. We would expect that as we become more like Jesus, we will become more godly, but our concept of godliness is inadequate. What really is godliness? In my work with hundreds of men in discipleship groups, I've noticed a sad but common phenomenon. Many fine Christian men are suffering unnecessarily from spiritual inferiority complexes. They are down on themselves and defeated. Not because they are trapped in sin, but simply because they fail to measure up to what they have been told is godliness, or deep spirituality.

A common thread runs through the fabric of these spiritual inferiority complexes. Most of these men have accepted a model of spirituality best described as *devotionalism*: a studious, quiet, reflective, contemplative spiritual life. I have talked with many men, like George, who says something like, "The wife—she's the spiritual one in the family." And he makes that assessment on the fact that his wife Nancy attends a Bible study group each week, having done her "homework"; she buys and reads lots of Christian books; and she prays with the kids each night as she puts them to bed. She also serves on the missions or Christian education committee at church.

On the other hand, when he tries to read a Christian book after working a long, hard day, he falls asleep. He helps out at a few church events like clean-up day, and he may go to the annual men's retreat. But he is not very deep into the Word, and he keeps his faith pretty much to himself at work.

Where did George and thousands of other Christian men get the idea that Nancy's devotionalism is the pinnacle of spirituality? Not from the Bible, I assure you! Most likely from the pulpits. Preachers, necessarily, spend many hours in quiet study and reflection, so that's the model they are most comfortable recommending. You meet God in the prayer closet or in your quiet time, they are fond of saying, as if God can't tolerate the dirt and the noise of the outside world.

Now this type of spirituality is wonderful. We admire those who use that approach to spiritual growth. Yet it is quite evident that Christianity wasn't put on the map by devotional types. At least as we define "devotional" today. The early Christians were devoted, true, but not to study and quiet time. They were devoted to a person, Jesus Christ their Lord. And he was an activist. And when they became empowered by the Holy Spirit, they became world changers.

Gauging Godliness

How do we know that many of the early Christians didn't study or practice "devotions" or "quiet time" as we know these habits? Two facts. Many, if not most, of the early believers were illiterate. Slaves comprised a large part of the early church. For those few who could read, only the Old Testament, written in Hebrew, was available. It spoke primarily to the Jewish minority of the church, not to the vast majority of Gentiles.[12] Second, even those who could read did not have ready access to the scriptures. This was true for centuries after Christ's life on earth. There were no family Bibles, pocket Testaments, or personal study Bibles. Scrolls were kept in synagogues (see Luke 4:16, 17), and New Testament books and letters were undoubtedly kept by house church leaders and apostles.

So these early Christians (and Old Testament believers) had to have a different standard of what constituted godliness. Certainly the teachings of Jesus handed down orally and later recorded by the Gospel writers were a major guide to godliness. Undoubtedly, Old Testament teaching became part of the formula, too. So, we would be wise to discover what they considered to be necessary for godliness. David, who is assumed to have been a devotional and introspective individual, gave this very down-to-earth, socially involved depiction of the godly person:

> *Lord, who may dwell in your sanctuary?*
> > *Who may live on your holy hill?*
> *He whose walk is blameless*
> > *and who does what is righteous,*
> *who speaks the truth from his heart*
> > *and has no slander on his tongue,*
> *who does his neighbor no wrong*
> > *and casts no slur on his fellow man,*
> *who despises a vile man*
> > *but honors those who fear the Lord,*
> *who keeps his oath*
> > *even when it hurts,*
> *who lends his money without usury*

> *and does not accept a bribe against the innocent.*
> *He who does these things will never be shaken.*

> (Psalm 15)

There are many Christians, like my friend George, who are living examples of Psalm 15, but because they're not devotional types they belittle their spirituality. Likewise, it is troublesome that many who do not do what is truly righteous—speak truth from the heart, etc.—feel smug in their spirituality because they abide by the quiet-time formula. Could it be that the standard of devotionalism as a gauge of godliness is a twenty-first century expression of Pharisaism?

These remarks are not intended to denigrate a devotional lifestyle. Spiritual disciplines are important; to be sure, we see Jesus withdrawing from the crowds for times of prayer. But if Jesus and the disciples had been only devotional, they would have died peacefully as good Jews. There would be no Christian church. It was as they took their spirituality into the world that their true righteousness confronted the corrupt religion and pagan state of their day. In the confrontation, God was able to speak and act.

But we must remember that prior to Pentecost, the disciples were more like spiritual wimps than warriors. And all too many of today's believers, in this post-pentecostal era, who have the opportunity of being filled with the Holy Spirit, live unempowered and defeated Christian lives, laboring under spiritual inferiority complexes that hold them down.

Have you ever opened the refrigerator and found a plastic bottle of Pepsi, looking forward to a tasty, cool drink, and then unscrewed the lid to find that the Pepsi had lost its fizz? Pepsi without fizz is just not the real thing. And Christian living without the filling of the Holy Spirit us not the real thing either. Conversion-only Christianity is like fizzless Pepsi. It's flat. Jesus meant for us to live carbonated lives, filled with the fizz of His Spirit. And He has provided that possibility which is experienced by millions of believers around the world, but also not experienced by many believers. In the next chapter we consider the manifestations of the Holy Spirit – the bubbles that prove the carbonation is there.

CHAPTER FOUR:
MANIFESTATIONS OF THE SPIRIT

On his fourth evening of preaching to a thousand students at a Christian college, Pastor James sensed God's Spirit revealing to him some messages for specific students in the audience. One by one he asked them to stand as he declared "words of knowledge" for them specifically.

He encouraged a young lady that she would soon receive the funds she needed to pay her tuition bill. To another young lady he said that God was calling her out to be an intercessor. He told another student not to worry about his transportation needs; God knew the situation and would take care of it. The student turned out to be a commuter! Another coed was told that she needed to be more understanding of her roommate who was going through some family problems. And to a young man he said God had heard his prayers for guidance about pursuing a career of ministry, and God would have him do so.

Reactions then and later among the students (and faculty) were divided. Some were thrilled that God had broken into their midst to give these words. Others were puzzled, never having experienced anything like this in real life; ok on TV maybe, but at our college? Many, however, were extremely skeptical, and saw it merely to be a show. Some were upset that the administration would allow a fraud like him to speak. Some of the leaders were skeptical of such "manifestations of the Spirit," and eager to ascertain the legitimacy of Pastor James' words. So a

53

female counselor, who easily engages students in conversation, went to the five students to hear what they thought about the speaker's "words of knowledge." Four of the students said that Pastor James was right on the money. Some of the four were astonished, because they were not previously sympathetic to anything charismatic. The fifth student wasn't as positive.

As stated in the previous chapter, the manifestations of the Spirit are evidences of God's presence in Christians ministering in various ways at different times. The manifestations Paul lists in 1 Corinthians 12 are not the only ways God manifests His Spirit, but the nine he lists are all legitimate expressions of the Holy Spirit today. They are:

> Word of wisdom
> Word of knowledge
> Faith
> Gifts of healing
> Effecting of miracles
> Prophecy
> Distinguishing of spirits
> Speaking in tongues
> Interpretation of tongues

Often, as in the story above, the manifestations of the Spirit occur in public gatherings of the body of Christ because their purpose is to edify the church. But Scripture does not restrict the manifestations to church services. Frequently in the ministry of Jesus while He was on earth, and today, God manifests His presence and power in small group settings and to individuals.

Some Cautions

Unlike with the spiritual gifts, a believer may exhibit any or all of the manifestations, as God chooses. Also, unlike the gifts, they are not permanently bestowed. For example, a person may be used in healing only once, if that is God's will. A person may have anointing for receiving and declaring words of knowledge in one context of ministry but not in others. A person may be able to interpret a tongues message only occasionally. The important issue here is to understand that God is adamant that He and only He will distribute the manifestations as He chooses. We cannot conjure them up at will. *But one and the same Spirit works all these things, distributing to each one individually just as He wills* (1 Corinthians 12:11; my underlining).

Unfortunately, one of the reasons some Christians are so mistrustful of manifestations is that these expressions are not always "of the Spirit." Fraudulent, self-initiated "manifestations" are not infrequent in many circles, and indeed, skeptics may well be right in saying the devil himself may cause havoc in the body of Christ by imitating the manifestations. However, such misuse should not cause us to toss out the beauty and value of true expressions of God. Paul makes it clear that we are not to despise prophetic utterances, and that we are to encourage the full expression of God's gifts and manifestations for edifying the body of Christ.

Because abuse of manifestations of the Spirit is so prevalent and destructive, in Appendix B I have shown the many statements Paul makes in 1 Corinthians in his pastoral correction of that church. If church leaders would insist that these biblical principles be followed, church life would be much more authentic, and there would be far fewer incidents of counterfeit *pneumatika*. And quite likely, the reputation of charismatic and Pentecostal churches would be better, and maybe more churches would engage in genuine, biblical body life.

While it seems clear from the wording Paul uses in listing the spiritual gifts in Romans 12 that the list of *charismata* is complete,[13] the list of manifestations in 1Corinthians 12: 8-10 may be merely suggestive of the ways God ministered through believers at Corinth. In Acts, as we have seen, when the Spirit filled people, there were other manifestations that occurred, such as boldness. For now, however, we will look at the ones Paul listed.

God can give any manifestation to any believer (or even unbeliever) He chooses. Generally, however, those who exercise *pneumatika* are Spirit-filled people who have yielded fully to the Holy Spirit and are eager for Him to use them in ministry.

Description of Manifestations of the Spirit

A **word of wisdom** is a message God imparts in a situation requiring clarification and divine perspective. In one sense every admonition in scripture is a word of wisdom because all scripture is inspired by God's Spirit (2 Timothy 3:16). Peter and John expressed a word of wisdom to the Sanhedrin when they were commanded *not to speak or teach at all in the name of Jesus. [They] replied, "Judge for yourselves whether it is right in God's sight to obey you rather than God. For we cannot help speaking about what we have seen and heard."* (Acts 4: 18-20)

A good example of a word of wisdom occurred shortly after the terrorists' attack on the World Trade Center in New York City. On September 13, 2001, Anne Graham Lotz, the daughter of the Reverend Billy Graham, appeared on CBS's Early Show. Jane Clayson interviewed her, and here is part of the transcript of that program.

> *Jane Clayson: I've heard people say, those who are religious, those who are not, if God is good, how could God let this happen? To that, you say?*

> *Anne Graham Lotz: I say God is also angry when he sees something like this. I would say also for several years now Americans in a sense have shaken their fist at God and said, God, we want you out of our schools, our government, our business, we want you out of our marketplace. And God, who is a gentleman, has just quietly backed out of our national and political life, our public life. Removing his hand of blessing and protection. We need to turn to God first of all and say, "God, we're sorry we have treated you this way and we invite you now to come into our national life. We put our trust in you." We have our trust in God on our coins; we need to practice it.*[14]

Anne's statement was so sharp and perceptive, so stunning as a response to a difficult question, that quite likely it was a message sent by God for the large audience to hear. Its wisdom is compelling—truly a word of wisdom.

A word of wisdom is not the same as wisdom. Human wisdom is a valuable resource. God was pleased that Solomon asked for wisdom to lead the people, and an example of that wisdom came soon after he received it. Two mothers of infants who lived in the same house came to Solomon seeking justice. One of them had accidentally suffocated her baby during the night, gotten up and exchanged the infants, and said the living one was hers. Solomon's stroke of wisdom was to suggest that the living baby be cut in half, one half for each woman. The woman of the living son immediately protested and said to give the child to the other woman. The other woman said to go ahead and divide the baby so it would belong to neither of them. Of course, this revealed to Solomon which one was the true mother. Human wisdom is a wonderful quality, but words of wisdom are pneumatic—they come directly from God. They are not part of a rational process, but of spiritual sensitivity and insight.

In the midst of an annual church meeting a debate (quarrel) broke out over whether the church should proceed with a building program. The new pastor was horrified as the voices became increasingly strident. He wondered whether he should have come to this church. As the meeting was beginning to get out of control, finally the young pastor said, "I make a motion that the meeting be adjourned, and that we table this issue for a year. We cannot build a church if we cannot behave like a church." That was a word of wisdom. In the intervening year all four families that protested the building project moved out of the area. At the next annual meeting, the proposal to build went through uncontested and within fifteen months, the congregation was enjoying new facilities.

Was this just human wisdom? It might have been had it come from one of the mature executives in the church. But the young pastor was stepping way out of character and expected protocol to give this word he was sure came from God.

A word of knowledge is a direct revelation from God that gives information needed in a ministry situation to communicate a message. The speaker of the word of knowledge would have no natural, human way of knowing that information. The example above about Pastor James' words of knowledge demonstrates that God is able to reveal factual details to a Spirit-filled believer about a person's situation. He will do it when he knows that the person will use that information for God's purposes and glory.

The woman at Jacob's well in Samaria was amazed when Jesus responded to her statement that she had no husband. He said, *You have well said, "I have no husband," for you have had five husbands, and the one whom you now have is not your husband....* (John 4:17,18).

Human knowledge, of course, is valuable, but as Paul wrote in 1 Corinthians 8:1, *Knowledge puffs up (or makes arrogant).* Human knowledge can be used for good or for evil. Remember, it was the tree of the knowledge of good and evil that produced the forbidden fruit which when eaten brought death into this world (Genesis 2:17).

Faith is one of the dominant words and concepts in Scripture, but in the context of 1 Corinthians 12, Paul uses the word to describe a specific kind of faith, a manifestation of the Spirit. This is not saving faith or basic belief, nor is it the general kind of trust that expects something to happen. These kinds of faith are surely gifts of God (see Ephesians 2:8 and Hebrews 11 as examples). The manifestation of faith, however, is a revelation from God that a certain thing will, indeed, happen. It is well beyond hope and trust; it is certainty.

Jesus demonstrated this kind of faith when He told Peter, James and John not to tell anyone about His transfiguration until after He had risen from the dead. He wasn't at this point prophesying He would rise, nor was it a hopeful kind of faith he was expressing; it was a statement of fact that a remarkable event would occur.

A memorable event occurred in my teenage years in the early 1960's watching my father exhibit the manifestation of faith in concert with his spiritual gift of giving. Dr. Gordon Anderson was speaking at our church, and gave an oblique hint in the message about a novel way of doing evangelism using filmed testimonies. I saw my dad flash five fingers to my mom and she nodded. After the service as they were shaking hands, my dad greeted Dr. Anderson by putting a check into his hand and saying, "Use this to buy the camera to start your television ministry." Later, I learned that the check was the $500 my folks had saved as down payment for a car. Several years later in New York I met Dr. Anderson who had gone on to develop Tele-Mission International. He told me that my dad's faith and gift gave him the assurance he needed to go ahead with this ministry, and he did use the money to buy his first video camera.

Gifts of healing are acts of grace that God chooses to do through human ministers by imparting this specific manifestation. Personally, I do not believe that this manifestation anymore than the others is permanently bestowed. Some individuals exhibit this ministry very frequently, combining it with the manifestations of faith and miracles. But not everyone to whom they minister is healed. This is not a criticism. Not every evangelistic sermon brings people to saving faith, either. God's will is not always known with certainty when we minister.

The gifts of healing that are manifestations of the Spirit are the same kind of healing that Jesus frequently performed. Now, it should be understood right away that Jesus is the only healer. Peter made it quite clear in telling the Jewish authorities in Acts 4:10, *let it be known to all of you, and to all the people of Israel, that by the name of Jesus Christ the Nazarene, whom you crucified, whom God raised from the dead—by this name this man stands here before you in good health.*

Sometimes the manifestation of healing is given first to the one who is ministering to the afflicted one; for example, it is not uncommon for the one praying to sense warmth in his or her hands. Other times the healing is given as a gift directly to the one needing it. An example of the first type occurred when Maryann, a new believer in Jesus Christ, was carried into my church office by her unbelieving fiancé. She had suffered from lower back pain for quite awhile, but the pain had now immobilized her. She had been treated medically, but had not received much help. Having read in the Bible about Jesus' power to heal and knowing our church believed in it, she asked us to pray for her.

It was a Saturday afternoon in New York when the elders gathered with me to anoint her with oil and to pray for her. Not long into the praying we sensed that God was present. We had an inner assurance that God would heal her. Right in the midst of a prayer, Maryann uttered loudly something about feeling heat in her back. She began crying with joy, as we kept praying. Finally, she grew impatient, jumped up from the couch and ran into the sanctuary to thank God for healing her. To this day I do not know whose faith activated the healing, but I do know who healed Maryann.

A few years ago in Idaho at a deeper life seminar Ben and I ended a ministry session asking people who wanted to be prayed for to receive the filling of the Holy Spirit to come forward. The first one to come was an elder whom I had met the previous day. I decided I would pray for him. Then a whole group of people came forward at once, and since I was already into prayer with the elder, they came to young Ben.

He had never seen a miraculous healing before, and that was the farthest thing from his mind. As he was ministering the Holy Spirit, a woman name Sherry, who did not come forward but who was seated in the second row right in the midst of Ben's prayer group, spoke up about her injured back. She said she had coped with much pain for five years since an accident on a motorcycle. She wanted God to heal her that day.

Ben plunged right in doing what he had seen done before but without positive results. He called for oil and prayed for her. She left that day exclaiming it was the first time in five years she felt no pain in her back. The next day, Sunday morning, she returned to testify in church that she was feeling great, and she had such energy and health the previous night that she cleaned the whole house. Later Ben confessed to me that he was totally surprised that she was healed, so it must have been someone else's faith. I suggested that it seemed that God had given her the gift of healing directly.

Miracles are manifested when God decides to break through natural order and do something that to us appears to be supernatural. Often He does this without human agency. Sometimes, however, He empowers humans to be His agent for doing the miraculous. Usually (I hesitate to say "always" because God doesn't live or act within the limits we prescribe), the focus on the miracle is to demonstrate the reality and presence of the kingdom of God for redemptive purposes. Sometimes God works miracles to stimulate belief. Other times it is to communicate a message of judgment, love, grace or power.

In one sense all the manifestations of the Spirit are miraculous. Some are more surprising and sensational than others, but when God shows up in human activity, by definition it is a supernatural event. A congregation touched by God's glory in worship is miraculous. A prophetic sermon that evokes repentance is miraculous. An answered prayer about a financial need is a miracle. Insight by a Christian counselor into a person's lifestyle of sin that is causing self-destructive behavior is miraculous. In truth, a miracle occurs any time the power and the presence of the kingdom of God override the damning effects of the fall and its sinful consequences.

The first century apostles were specifically chosen to be agents of miracles, but God hasn't limited Himself to them. Physical healing is probably the most frequent demonstration of the miraculous in our day. I suspect, however, that many of the fortuitous "circumstances" of life and history have the fingerprints of God all over them. In my own experience, I have seen my life take totally unexpected U-turns, where the hand of God was so evident.

From God's perspective, I suppose, there is no distinction between His acts—those that seem natural to us and those that seem supernatural. On the continuum of events in history there may be no clear demarcation. I have seen in so-called third world cultures some extraordinary spiritual phenomena that in my own culture would be debated. Some would

61

describe demonic manifestations as merely psychological gimmickry, while others allow for mysteries beyond our experiences.

In looking for examples of manifestations of miracles that are not healings or deliverances (a type of healing), most of what I would call a miracle others may describe as being merely natural coincidences. I have not seen water separated in a sea, walked on water, or turned water into wine. I have not seen a flaming bush not consumed, or chariots of fire, or tongues of fire.

But I have seen alcoholics and drug addicts delivered; I have seen demonized witches surrender to Jesus; I have seen hard-hearted, cynical administrators soften in response to prayer to make surprisingly faith-filled decisions.

Even though events that fit the strictest definition of miracle are not in huge abundance in our culture today, God is free to act as He chooses. In southern Africa during the past few years, God has raised a number of people from the dead through the ministry of Roland and Heidi Baker.[15]

In August 2005 while in China I heard through a translator a story from several house church leaders about their missionary ministries into the western provinces. They told about several spectacular healings. And then they told about going to a village out in the desert where rainfall was very rare and water was so scarce many people washed their face only once a year and had never fully bathed. When these house church leaders arrived and began telling about Jesus, whom no one in the village had ever heard about, rain began falling. They soon left, not knowing if anyone believed in Jesus. Some weeks later they decided to return, and again as they spoke, it began raining. Some people thought maybe these strangers brought the rain, and a few folks trusted in Jesus. A while later the ministers returned again and this time it poured, and so did the blessing of God. Almost everyone in the village became a follower of Jesus. Now, according to my Chinese hosts, that village gets frequent rainfalls, and is an oasis in the desert.

For many years I have kept a journal of miracles that have been part of my personal life, not counting many ministry miracles. While I am sure there have been many more, thus far I have recorded forty-five. Four were dramatic healings, six were deliverances from death or serious injury, eleven were surprising leadings or guidance that changed the direction of my life. Ten were specific revelations or words of knowledge, eleven were general gifts of grace that were more than coincidental, and one each of an amazing conversion, a return to faith, and a number of demonic deliverances.

Prophecy is the most complicated manifestation because it is also listed as a *charisma*—a gift—in Romans 12:6. "Prophet" is also in the Ephesians 4 list of church leaders. And prophesying and tongues were obviously at the heart of the divisions in the church at Corinth. While prophesying is a basic orientation toward ministry as a spiritual gift, it also is an activity exercised by some in the public assemblies. Paul gave specific guidelines for its proper use, but was adamant about defending prophecy as a legitimate and important ministry in the body of Christ.

Several kinds of verbal presentations may be considered prophecy. The primary meaning is to declare forth a word from God that engages the human will and requires obedient response. Usually the theme of prophesying concerns the need to know and live by God's standard of righteousness. Preaching may be prophetic in this sense. Writing may be prophetic. Music may also be prophetic. For example, I remember a song by Larry Norman called *Everybody's Dressing Up Jesus*, written during the 1970's era of the Jesus People. Norman chides both the established church and the uncommitted new Jesus Freaks for fashioning Jesus to suit their preferences. Some, he said, had Jesus wearing a conservative, gray suit, while others had Him in beard and sandals. The prophetic theme was that we were all prone to create Jesus in our own image, the reverse of God creating us in His image.

Another type of prophecy is foretelling, or predicting. Obviously, Jesus was Spirit-filled, and so He prophesied many times, like when He told Peter that he would betray Him three times before the cock crowed

(John 13:38). Peter also prophesied when he told Sapphira that because she and her husband Ananias had lied to God about giving to the Lord all the funds from a sale, the same men who had just buried her husband would carry out dead, too. (Acts 5:7-10)

Even though prophesying can evoke a lot of discomfort, either because of the message, the messenger or the supernatural element it assumes, Paul insisted that this ministry has an important role to play in the life of the church. Rather than stifling prophecy,[16] we must make sure that the spirit of the prophet is properly submitted to other prophets,[17] so that no one can exercise undue influence or deceive the body of Christ with counterfeit messages. Prophecy is one of the easier manifestations to imitate and that is sometimes done by satanic influence in clairvoyant messengers, such as fortune tellers and people claiming to have extrasensory perception, which perhaps is why next in Paul's list is….

Discernment of spirits is a manifestation that at times appears to be supernatural and at times appears to be simply human discernment. What Paul has in mind here, I believe, is the ability to sort through supernatural phenomena and know what is of God and what is a fraudulent imitation of the enemy. The prevalence of demonic spirits is widely debated, but unless we believe that Jesus was deluded or that at some time during the past two thousand years demons have become extinct, we must reject the modernist worldview that says all departures from normal human behavior are due to either chemical or psychological imbalance. While demonic activity and influence may be more apparent in so-called third world nations than in the modern West, those who have eyes to see are aware that Satan is alive and active in the first world also.

Jesus commissioned his disciples to "preach, heal and cast out demons." We see them doing these things in the book of Acts. For example, Acts 16:16 tells the story about a slave girl in Philippi who kept following Paul. He discerned the evil spirit in her and cast it out, speaking directly to the spirit.

God enables those filled with the Holy Spirit to have manifestations of discernment that go beyond mere diagnosis. The Apostles John and Paul wrote about the role of antichrist in the latter days. We have good reason to believe that as this evil influence multiplies, more believers will manifest the Holy Spirit's insights into the presence and practices of the evil one.

In February 2004 I led a team of four Americans to minister in Nigeria. We had been invited by a man known as Apostle Paul Taiwo Adenuga, founding pastor of Faith Revival Church in Lagos. During our five evening crusade we saw this young man exhibit spiritual discernment and power beyond anything we had experienced in the United States. I kept a journal so I could write a trip report; the next two paragraphs are extracted from that report. As you read, keep in mind that we witnessed these things personally. I think they make the point about discernment of spirits, and how God uses this manifestation.

Apostle Paul preached on Acts 3:19; his theme was repentance. He called people up to be delivered from spiritual bondage. In particular, he asked the Holy Spirit to fall on two witches he sensed were in the crowd of about 5000 people. We were amazed by the boldness of Paul. He said that these two women had washed their private parts and cooked their husbands' meals in the blood (in a superstitious effort to block their husbands from marrying other wives, as polygamy is rather common there). Eventually, the two women came forward and confessed their sins.

Later, Apostle Paul prayed for the fire of God to come on demonized people, and we experienced a crazy event of ushers carrying to the front about forty people that had fallen over. Most just lay still and quiet; others thrashed around, but none cried out. Some actually vomited out the oppression. Paul did everything he could to avoid sensationalism, but to deal with the problems. Whether in deliverance or praying for healing, he would not allow folks to touch others, but merely to pray. None of us had ever seen such a display of spiritual authority at work.

Presumably, God can give anyone the discernment of spirits, but quite likely those who receive such manifestations have a worldview that understands and "sees" into the spirit world. Those with the spiritual gift of prophecy may be most likely to exhibit this manifestation because of their keen spiritual antennae.

Speaking in tongues was one of the main ways that God manifested the filling of the Holy Spirit in the early church. As we saw in the previous chapter, three of the times that individuals or groups were filled with the Holy Spirit they spoke in tongues. At other times, other manifestations occurred, but in Jerusalem at Pentecost, at Caesarea with Cornelius and at Ephesus the believers had the evidence of their Spirit filling as they spoke in tongues.

It is not our purpose here to describe the phenomenon known as *glossalalia*, or to defend it or debate it. Clearly, many believers today practice this manifestation. Scripture seems to indicate that there are at least two kinds of tongues speaking. Tongues messages may be given in the public gathering of believers, but they must be interpreted. Praying in tongues is also indicated in Scripture to be a valid spiritual exercise (1 Corinthians 14:13, 14).

Paul indicated that he spoke in tongues more than any of the Corinthian believers (1 Corinthians 14:18), although he wrote that in the context of downplaying its importance relative to prophesying. He also insisted that use of this manifestation should be limited to two or three speakers in one meeting. See Appendix B for further description of the proper use of tongues.

Some people talk about having the gift of tongues. By our biblical analysis of gifts and manifestations, it would appear that speaking in tongues is a manifestation, not a gift. Therefore, it is not necessarily permanent. This might help some people understand why they have spoken in tongues in the past but have ceased doing so. None of the manifestations are available "on demand." Praying in tongues may be different, however. Praying in tongues is not mentioned in Scripture in the list of gifts or manifestations, but there are a number of references that give evidence that praying in tongues was practiced and accepted in the early church.[18] Being a type of prayer, like intercession or petition, praying in tongues is probably always available.

Quite likely, people of all kinds of spiritual gifts speak in tongues. Some Pentecostal groups have maintain that speaking in tongues is the one and only evidence that a person is filled with the Holy Spirit, or that it is the initial physical evidence. I think it is impossible to justify this belief either from Scripture or experience. However, the Pentecostals have done a service to the whole Church by insisting that when a person is filled with the Holy Spirit, he or she ought to expect something to happen. I believe that scripture indicates that any one of the manifestations is an adequate evidence of the filling.

Interpretation of tongues is the final manifestation listed in 1 Corinthians 12. As the wording implies, it is directly related to speaking in tongues. Paul made it very clear in 1 Corinthians 14:5 and 28 that tongues messages spoken in the public gathering of the church must be interpreted. Verse 5 implies that the one who has spoken in tongues may also provide the interpretation. Verse 28 implies that normally another person should be the interpreter.

One member of my prayer group told me that he had experienced all the manifestations of the Spirit except interpretation of tongues. Several weeks later a man in his church asked to be prayed for and anointed for healing. During the prayer time another man very sensitively asked the rest of the group if they minded if he prayed in tongues. Everyone agreed it would be all right. So, my friend quietly prayed, "Lord, please help me to interpret Bob's prayer."

At first, he told me, he was concentrating on the "words," trying to translate as a rational process. Then he just relaxed and listened for impressions in his spirit. After Bob finished praying, my friend had a very strong sense of the gist of the prayer and said to the man who was seeking the healing, "The Lord has said, 'My mercy is with you; my compassion is with you. I will be with you through the surgery'." Immediately, the one being prayed for said, "That's exactly what I sensed the Lord was saying." They looked to Bob, who just smiled and nodded. It was the first time Bob had prayed in tongues in front of anyone, and the first time my friend had interpreted.

Other Manifestations?

Does the Holy Spirit manifest the presence of Jesus through only the nine manifestations listed in 1 Corinthians 12:8-10? From the text and other uses of the word *phanerosis* there is no reason to believe these are the only manifestations. We have seen in Acts that early believers, after they were filled with the Holy Spirit, experienced boldness (Peter), revelation (Stephen), exaltation (Samaritans), authority to bind (Paul), and joy (the disciples). Other common experiences evident in those filled with the Holy Spirit are sincere worship, sacrifice, intercession, shaking, weeping, laughing, and falling before the Lord (which some call being slain in the Spirit, which is not biblical terminology, but is an experience seen frequently in Scripture when one was personally encountered by an angel or the Lord. It is also seen in John's vision of heaven in Revelation.) Certainly it is possible to "fake" these manifestations, but that does not nullify the validity of all such experiences. Undoubtedly, there are many more manifestations.

Dr. A. W. Tozer recognized the validity of spiritual experiences that are not explicitly seen in the Bible. No doubt, as a great worshipper, Tozer experienced the manifestations of Jesus frequently. He seemed to allow for a manifestation that many evangelicals debunked in the 1990's, holy laughter.

> *Now I say that worship is subject to degrees of perfection and intensity. There have been those who worshiped God to the place where they were in ecstasies of worship. I once saw a man kneel at an altar, taking Communion. Suddenly he broke into holy laughter. This man laughed until he wrapped his arms around himself as if he was afraid he would burst just out of sheer delight in the presence of Almighty God. A few times I have seen other people rapt in an ecstasy of worship where they were carried away with it, and I have also heard some simple hearted new converts*

saying "Abba Father." So worship is capable of running from the very simple to the most intense and sublime.[19]

Dr. Tozer also expected divine revelation to continue, as seen in this poignant statement:

I believe that much of our religious unbelief is due to a wrong conception of and a wrong feeling for the Scriptures of Truth. A silent God suddenly began to speak a book and when the book was finished lapsed into silence again forever. Now we read the book as the record of what God said when He was for the brief time in a speaking mood. With notions like that in our heads how can we believe? The facts are that God is not silent, has never been silent... He is by nature continuously articulate.[20]

Keep Your Focus

Even though it is important to recognize, experience and minister the manifestations of the Spirit, they are not meant to be objects of our attention. We must keep our eyes on Jesus, and allow His Spirit to work in and through us as He chooses. When we seek sensational experiences, as Peter did on the Mount of Transfiguration (Luke 9:33), hopefully, the Lord will gently rebuke us and return our focus to the Lord of glory.

CHAPTER FIVE:
WHAT ABOUT SPIRITUAL GIFTS?

In the mid-1990s, totally unaware of what was brewing in his own church, Pastor Brooks decided it would be good to have an elders' and wives' retreat with a guest speaker. So Betzi and I found ourselves driving to the Midwest glad for the opportunity to be away together and looking forward to a weekend of ministry together. The Pastor left it to me to decide on a topic and theme for the retreat.

Two decades earlier in our ministry we were deep into the topic of spiritual gifts and had explored the topic from every imaginable angle in the church we were serving. We hadn't thought much about or done much with that topic since then, so I was surprised when we sensed the Lord leading us to teach about spiritual gifts during the retreat.

The thrust of the seminar was not just to understand the gifts, but for each person to discover his or her gifting. After three two-hour sessions, all of the elders and wives, including the pastoral couple, were ready to express what they believed was their primary spiritual gift. In cases where people identified more than one gift we worked through some exercises to help them narrow it down to one primary gift.

Ten elders and wives were present. Here is what we found out about the elders. The head elder and organizer of the retreat had the gift of mercy, two of them had the gift of serving, one was a giver, one was an exhorter and five were administrators. Not one sensed that he had the gift of teaching or prophesying. Pastor Brooks, however, was clearly a prophet. He and his wife discerned this to be true, and all the elders and wives saw it to be true also.

After the retreat as we returned to the town where the church was located, our host couple said we had no idea how revolutionary the seminar was. What we didn't know, and what the pastor didn't know was that his ministry at that church was about to conclude. Our host told us that several of the elders were ready to talk with the district superintendent about replacing Pastor Brooks because of his poor administrative and pastoral skills. Everyone was happy about his preaching and the strong, godly example he was. They delighted in his wife and her great compassion and strong ministry with the children of the church. They appreciated their ten years of ministry, but believed that there were areas of the leadership in the church that needed to be strengthened.

In fact, they confided, if it were not for the head elder, and what they now understood to be his strong gift of mercy, the change would already have been made. Our host, one of the administrators, said he now saw that they had in their group a lot of gifting among the lay leaders that could and should readily supplement the pastor's ministry, if he would allow them to serve in their gifting. He planned to talk with the pastor and head elder about it that week.

I did not hear from either the pastor or the church for a few years. Then I chanced to see Pastor Brooks at a conference. I asked where he was serving and how his ministry was going. His response both surprised and blessed me, "Oh, I'm still at the same church. The Lord is blessing us, and our elders and wives are providing excellent leadership."

Not all stories will end quite as happily as this one, but it is evidence that understanding and using spiritual gifts wisely in the local church can have a powerful, positive effect.

Gifts For the Church

One of the great liabilities of the modern church is that we tend to view every topic far too individualistically. Many Christians want to be baptized and filled with the Spirit so that they can showcase their individual ministry. Simon the Magician (Acts 8:9-24) provides ample warning against this kind of individualistic motivation. Similarly, some people want to know their spiritual gift to enhance their own life and ministry, when God wants us to know and use our gift for the benefit of the body of Christ.

Being filled with the Holy Spirit is crucial for ministry effectiveness, but knowing and excelling in one's own special area of gifting will bring greatest glory to God, blessing to the Church and personal satisfaction. You might say, "Well, why wouldn't being filled with the Spirit be enough? Why bother about spiritual gifts?" By response I'd like to use an analogy that plays on the word for spirit—*pneuma,* which also means breath or wind.

Suppose you are a gifted musician, and an orchestra is looking for someone to play a wind instrument. You volunteer, saying that you have played since you were ten years old and have performed in many bands and orchestras. The orchestra conductor asks what kind of wind instrument you play and you respond that you play the clarinet. He responds that they need a bassoonist. You reply, well I'm very experienced; I have great wind control; I read music very well, and I'd be willing to give it a try. Only if he were very ignorant or very desperate would the conductor consent.

How often in the local church do we completely ignore spiritual gifting as we seek to place people in ministries? Whether or not people have gifting, training or experience, we seem so eager to place them in roles just to fill slots. No wonder so many churches have to reach up just to see mediocre. As one cynic says, they suffer from delusions of adequacy.

However, when believers know their spiritual gift, know how, where and when to use it, and are filled with the Holy Spirit, genuine, effective, impacting ministry occurs. That is why it is important to consider spiritual gifts in the context of spiritual empowerment. (For now, I will use the word *gift* in the singular; we will discuss this issue later.)

A few key preliminary ideas are important to know:
* Every Christian has a spiritual gift, which is imparted and resident with the Holy Spirit when one becomes born again. For many, that gift lies dormant and will be activated when they get involved with ministry. When believers are baptized with the Holy Spirit, their gifting accelerates toward maturity.
* It is important for you to know your spiritual gift, as seen above in the example of Pastor Brooks and his church.
* The words gift, grace and joy are related etymologically. *Char* is the root word and means joy. *Charis* means grace, and *charisma* is singular for gift. *Charismata* is plural, and might be translated "things of grace."
* Some people wonder how gifts are related to natural abilities. God may bless and use a natural gift as your spiritual gift. The Apostle Peter may be an example of this. He was clearly a leader before Pentecost, although he failed several times. After he was filled with the Holy Spirit, his leadership matured greatly.
* As stated above, the purpose of spiritual gifts is not for self-satisfaction. God designed each gift to edify the Church and enhance its ministry both internally and externally. While in His goodness God delights to give us joy as we minister, our greatest joy will come as we see blessing in the lives of others.

Understanding Spiritual Gifts

How many spiritual gifts are there, and what are they? This question is often debated, and many books have been written assuming anywhere from seven to twenty-two spiritual gifts. The confusion is due to not seeing an important nuance in Scripture.

In Scripture there are four lists of "gifts" of the Holy Spirit. This can be somewhat confusing because the gifts are not identical in the four passages. One of the lists is in Ephesians 4, where Paul wrote about people who are gifts from God to the church. The Greek word for "gifts" used here is *domata*, not *charismata*. They are the people who serve in various functions or offices of the Church, universal and local: apostles, prophets, evangelists, pastors, and teachers. Since it is obvious in that passage that the gifts are people, we do not necessarily refer to them as gifts of the Holy Spirit, meaning endowments or abilities given for ministry.

I believe much of the confusion about spiritual gifts is due to a mistranslation of 1 Corinthians 12:1. The Greek text actually says, *Now about spiritual (things) [pneumatika]* or *that which is spiritual.* Paul did not use *charismata,* the word for gifts. You will see in some of the more literal translations, such as the NASV or KJV, that the word "gifts" is supplied and printed in italics, meaning the translators were aware that the word does not appear in the Greek. Some translations, like the NIV, ignore this important distinction, probably because the interpreters have been conditioned to view the list in verses 8-10 as gifts, even though they are specifically called manifestations.

In verses 4-6 Paul gives three categories of *pneumatika: charismata, diakonia,* and *energemata* – gifts, ministries and effects. Verses 8-10, the manifestations, refer to the effects of the Holy Spirit. And it is evident that the Corinthian believers were having some problems with the manifestations, not the gifts, of the Spirit, for that is what Paul writes about in chapters 12 and 14 of 1 Corinthians.

First Corinthians 12 gives two lists of *pneumatika.* Those in verses 8-10 are *manifestations* of the Spirit, which we examined in the last chapter. (One of the manifestations has attached to it the word *gifts,* namely "gifts of healing.") The manifestations of the Spirit are evidences of God's presence in Christians ministering in various ways at different times. The manifestations Paul mentions may not be the only ways believers can manifest the Spirit, but the nine he lists are all legitimate expressions of the Holy Spirit today.

First Corinthians 12:28-30 also gives a list, which features some functions like those in Ephesians 4, and some manifestations like those in verses 8-10. Paul's point in verses 28-30 was to emphasize the variety of spiritual ministries and the certainty that the church needs the ministry of all the members. Again, this list is not explicitly called spiritual gifts.

In only one place in Scripture is there a listing under the name *charismata*, and that is Romans 12:6-8, where the Apostle Paul mentions prophecy, serving, teaching, exhorting (or encouraging), giving, organizing (or leading) and mercy. While each believer has one of these gifts and while we usually minister from the basis of that gift, we are not limited to spiritual gifts when we serve God. He also gives us opportunities to serve through a variety of ministries and manifestations. Hence, the distinction between gifts, ministries and effects may not be too important. The primary difference is that a gift is permanently resident in the believer, while manifestations occur for specific occasions. While the manifestations of the Spirit may seem to be more spectacular, the gifts of the Spirit are more foundational to the life of the church.

Only One Gift?

From the context of the list of *charismata* in Romans 12 and in several other biblical passages, it is evident that the apostle teaches that each believer has only one spiritual gift. We may have many ministries and manifestations of the Spirit, but they will all flow out of one primary spiritual gift from those listed in Romans 12:6-8.

Many believers do not want to accept the idea that they have only one spiritual gift, but here is further textual evidence that this is true. Romans 12:4 compares spiritual gifts to members of a body. This would be a poor analogy if one person could be many, or even two, organs of the body. Romans 12:3-8 teaches that each believer is to concentrate fully on the gift God has given him. This would not be possible if we have more than one spiritual gift.

Peter separated gifts into speaking and serving gifts but emphasized that *Each one should use whatever spiritual gift he has received....* The noun for gift is singular (1 Peter 4:10, 11). Paul instructed Timothy not to *neglect the spiritual gift within you,* (1 Timothy 4:14), assuming only one gift. Again, gift is singular. One would think that with all Paul was depending upon and expecting from Timothy, he would have tried to impart more than one gift to the young pastor of the church at Ephesus.

Finally, a corporate and personal benefit is that having only one spiritual gift helps keep us that much more dependent on each other and Christ, and keeps us properly humble (Romans 12:3).

I'm not too sure how important this issue is. Surely it should not become a divisive issue. Hopefully, there will never be any church splits or new denominations formed because of dissension on the singularity or plurality of spiritual gifts. But what is important is that we know at least one gift of the Holy Spirit within us and learn to exercise biblically the manifestations of the Holy Spirit in ministry. If a believer wants to believe he or she has more than one gift, and understands the distinction between gifts and manifestations, that's fine. But, in my opinion, biblically, that position cannot be justified. Sometimes, however, different understandings of the *pneumatika* can lead to serious dissensions in a local church, as in this true story from my first pastorate.

Trauma in the Hospital and the Church

The church was in total torturous turmoil. A young father of three beautiful children had been stricken with a kidney disease requiring him to undergo dialysis three days each week. Tim had been a very active deacon in the church and an avid participant in town events. Everyone knew him, and respect for the church from the folks in the village leaped forward when Tim became a Christian and was transformed. In many ways he was the church's best ambassador to the town folks.

Tim was able to have the dialysis at home, but these experiences were very hard on the family. The young children didn't understand what was going on, and Tim's strong spiritual gift of server and Jan's gift of organizer had them in reverse roles during each six-hour session. Fortunately, when we helped Tim and Jan each discover and understand their spiritual gift, they got along a lot better. (And, by the way, I've seen dozens of marriages repaired when the spouses know each other's spiritual gift.)

After many months of waiting, at last the good news came that there was a suitable donor kidney available for him. Although the surgery was somewhat risky, for Tim there was no question that he would go through with it. He had become so demoralized by his life of inactivity and dependency on others.

Now he lay comatose in a Brooklyn hospital, having received a successful kidney implant. Bodily functions were fine. What had not been anticipated was the eruption of a blood vessel aneurysm in his brain, which the doctors suspected was congenital.

Upset by this news, the church began praying. Certainly God would not tarnish His reputation or ours by taking Tim. Surely this was the work of the devil, and enough fasting, praying and trusting would gain the victory.

During the week as Tim lay unconscious and on life-support, the church was comforted by many prophetic words from some of the charismatic members of the congregation. We were also unceasingly exhorted by a Pentecostal brother to build up our faith because God always responds to positive faith. When healings do not occur, it is because we lack faith, he told us.

As a young pastor and close friend of Tim and his family, I was aware of the dynamics in the church, but spent most of the week at the hospital with Jan and the kids. With Jan's eager permission, I asked the elders to join me in anointing with oil and praying for Tim's healing. We were doing everything we knew to do. My own faith was strong, but truthfully, I was not sure what God intended to do.

When Jan and Tim's parents agreed to "pull the plug" after several days of no brain waves, we committed him to God's grace and reaffirmed our trust in God to do the right thing, though we were so deeply bereaved. Jan had one comforting thought. We were in the midst of a building project, and the elders and deacons agreed that Tim's urn would be placed in the cornerstone. We all thought it was a fitting image in two ways: Tim was a solid strength in the life of the church, and Jesus is the cornerstone and Tim was literally with Him now.

The after-effects in our evangelically pluralistic church were quietly devastating. The charismatically and pentecostally inclined members tended to judge the church for not having enough faith. The more generic evangelicals tended to judge the charismatics and Pentecostals for being false prophets and having false theology. Mind you, all this was an undercurrent. Our love for Tim and his family inhibited us from letting this become a public issue. I wish I could say this story had a happy ending. Maybe had they had a more spiritually experienced pastor at the time, it would have been handled better.

Paul's Adolescent Church

Such is life in a church marked by a variety of spiritual orientations. Such was the church at Corinth. It was young, vibrant, gifted and immature. In many ways it was an adolescent church—complete with cliques and heroes. I believe that all the issues (problems) Paul addressed in his letters to the Corinthians must be seen in the context of the biggest issue Paul tackled in 1 Corinthians 1, namely, divisions in the church. He accused the church of "party spirit;" members saying they were of Paul, Cephas, Apollos or Christ.

Imagine for a moment what these groups would have been like. Those of Paul, the Apostle to the Gentiles, were probably new converts who came to Christ right out of paganism. They may have witnessed Paul's apostolic ministry of miracles, and were open to spiritual innovation. They appreciated their new life and the freedom of the gospel not to have to live by a religious code. Quite likely, they were tolerant of the spiritual imperfections of others, including new believers.

Those who followed Cephas, or Peter, the Apostle to the Jews, were steeped in Mosaic law, and continued to observe those scruples, believing that the way of Jesus was not a departure from Judaism, but an amendment. Quite likely they were sympathetic with Judaizers, who insisted that Gentile converts should submit to circumcision and come to Christianity as proselyte Jews, being properly Torah observant.

Apollos was known as a Jewish intellectual, very skilled in what today we call apologetics. (See Acts 18:24, 25.) He could present the case for the messiahship of Jesus very convincingly. His followers were probably educated Jews and Gentiles, who delighted in the rational aspects of the Christian faith. They probably evaluated every practice by what Scripture said, and may not have been too sympathetic with the enthusiastic embracing of some of the more experiential aspects of Christian body life.

Certainly those who said they were of Christ must have been above reproach, right? If so, why did Paul mention them with the others who needed correction? One possibility might be that they were self-righteous and independent in spirit. Admittedly, this is conjecture, but every pastor knows people like this, so it would not be surprising that they existed even in the first century. They may have been judgmental of the spiritual liabilities of Paul, Peter, Apollos and those who followed their teachings. This spirit would infect the congregation with the kind of cynicism Paul had to address in defending his apostleship in his second letter to the Corinthians.

So this is the backdrop to chapters 12-14 that address the issue of *pneumatika*. In these chapters Paul was trying to correct a situation in which the manifestations were being abused. Keep that in mind, and we will return to 1 Corinthians after examining more carefully the *charismata* that Paul listed in Romans.

You might be wondering: biblically, how do manifestations relate to gifts of the Holy Spirit? Intrigued by this question, I have explored and found (for me) new insight on gifts and manifestations, focusing on three words.

Three Important Words

The most general New Testament Greek word for gift is *dorea*. In Acts 2:38 the Apostle Peter uses this word during his Pentecostal sermon, inviting his listeners to receive the gift of the Holy Spirit. In John 4:10 Jesus told the woman at the well in Samaria that if she knew the gift of God and who was asking for water, she would ask Him and He would give her living water. Peter admonished Simon the Magician who offered to pay money for the gift of God when Simon saw the spiritual power Peter exercised (Acts 8:20). Later Peter and all his circumcised friends were amazed when they saw that the gift of the Holy Spirit had been poured out on the Gentiles (10:45); the same word for gift is used in 11:17 when Peter was explaining this impartation. Surprisingly, *dorea* is the word in Ephesians 4:7 referring to four or five ecclesiastical offices (apostle, prophet, evangelist, pastor / teacher). Another use of this general word for gift is found in Hebrews 6:4 where the author talks about those who have *tasted of the heavenly gift* and have partaken of the Holy Spirit.

A better-known Greek word for gift is *charisma (ta),* which is derived from the root word *charis*, which means grace. A *charisma* is literally a thing of grace. Often the word is found in combination with *pneumatika*, when it means spiritual gift. In Romans 1:11 Paul stated that he was eager to visit the Roman Christians to impart a spiritual gift to them. In 11:29 he assured them that the gifts and callings of God are irrevocable. In 12:6 he lists the seven spiritual gifts—a list which is literally the only one in Scripture that uses the term *spiritual gifts*. In 1 Corinthians *charisma (ta)* occurs several times. In 1:7 Paul wrote to the believers in Corinth that they were not lacking any spiritual gift. In chapter 12 the word is used several times:
- Verse 4 – *there are varieties of gifts*
- Verses 9, 28, 30 – *gifts of healing*
- Verse 31 – *desire the greater gifts*

Paul used the same word twice in writing to Timothy. In 1 Timothy 4:14 he told his young protégé, *Do not neglect the spiritual gift within you.* In 2 Timothy 1:6 he said, *Kindle afresh the gift of God within you.*

81

The Apostle Peter did not develop the concept fully but did admonish his readers, *As each one has received a gift, employ it in serving one another* (1 Pet 4:10). Notice here and in the passages in Timothy that the language indicates only one *charisma* per person. The same assumption is seen in the imagery Paul used in Romans and 1 Corinthians.

The third important word in this study is *phanerosis*, meaning manifestation, which we considered in depth in chapter four.

Charismata

In writing to the Romans Paul was laying down his most basic teaching. First he gave his understanding of the nature of man, and then described the gospel of Jesus Christ, before turning to the work of the Holy Spirit. Romans 12 contains Paul's most basic teaching on the spiritual gifts. By emphasizing the gifts, I am not expressing any reservation about the validity and importance of the manifestations of the Spirit. In fact, part of the concern of this book is that so many evangelical Christians have settled for a bland spirituality that excludes the manifestations of the Spirit. But understanding the gifts is important in our understanding of the work of the Holy Spirit.

We will look at the seven gifts that Paul lists in Romans, but before doing so, I'd like to point out two related issues. First, all the spiritual gifts are available to males and females. Regardless of the pronoun I may use, please understand that the gift applies to both genders. To make the point, I will alternate the pronouns among the seven gifts. Second, a person's ministry may not be the same as his or her spiritual gift. Not all who teach, for example, have the gift of teaching. I will use the term *teacher* to refer to one with that gift, and the same applies to the other gifts.

Prophecy

In our day there is great misunderstanding about the role of prophecy. Many consider the gift of the prophet to be the ability to peer down the tunnels of the future and make predictions. The prophet, however, is not a Christian crystal-ball gazer. The primary function of the prophet is to speak forth the message of God to his own people about their own lives in their own situation. The prophet is the one who begins his message with "Thus says the Lord." He is the one who brings God's truth powerfully to the attention of Christians. He is the one who is persuasive in speech and who has unusual insight into motives of his hearers.

Generally, the prophet is zealous for righteousness, for he cannot tolerate partial good or partial righteousness. He tends to minister most effectively to groups and is not always effective in personal relationships. Often a prophet will give his message through a preaching ministry, but not always. Many times the prophet will speak very unexpectedly and his message may seem to be critical and judgmental.

A prophet needs to be careful that he does not unnecessarily wound those who are especially sensitive. He also needs to be careful that he does not become proud about his abilities to discern and persuade.

Earlier I mentioned Pastor Brooks from a church in the Midwest, a man whose gift was prophecy. He was appreciated in his church for delivering strong sermons that upheld the glory of God, His standards of righteousness, and the need for the church to be pure. He was not compromising in his presentations. People could always count on him to have unusual insights into issues that most people were not aware of—issues that could damage the reputation of the Lord or the church.

Dr. A. W. Tozer, whom I have quoted earlier, was known as a prophet. In fact, the biography about him is named *A. W. Tozer: Twentieth Century Prophet*. His messages and books gave strong warnings about theological modernism, and pointed people toward a deeper experience with God. Hundreds of thousands have read *The Pursuit of God* and *Knowledge of the Holy*.

83

Serving

The server has quite a different ministry in the body of Christ. Always eager to show the love of Christ by meeting very practical human needs, she seems to have a special sensitivity to the personal needs of others and is able to overlook her own personal discomfort in order to meet those needs. Often she is a very busy person, and has a difficult time refusing any ministry. The server wants so much to help people that she cannot easily say no.

She also likes to accomplish her tasks quickly to sense the joy of the one whom she has served and helped. Because she is eager to help other people, the server may appear to be brash and forward—perhaps a bit pushy. Others may feel that she does not really address the spiritual needs of a person but merely the practical, everyday-life needs. Like the prophet, she also must be aware of the temptation to be proud of her good deeds. The server functions best when she learns not to depend upon the praise of other people about her ministries.

Servers, like my friend Tim who died of the brain aneurysm, are quick to volunteer for practical projects like clean-up days at the church. They will be the first ones there and the last to leave, and they will tackle jobs that others do not want to do. We get the word "deacon" from the Greek word for server, and I still have warm memories of watching Tim move around the church making sure everything was in order—the heat set correctly, all the light bulbs working, the offering being counted after the service, enough chairs and tables set up for every function, and so on. From the parsonage, often I would see Tim's truck at the church after work, and I'd know he would be fixing something, and no one else would ever know of his extra work, and that was just fine with him.

My mother was a server *par excellence.* She loved being a hostess, enjoyed leading the Christian Women's Club, remembered everyone's birthday and anniversary, and never tired of driving her children to after-school events. She also led the Tabitha group at church, which was appropriate because Tabitha was clearly a server, as we see in Acts 9:36-39; *this woman was abounding with deeds of kindness and charity, which she continually did*. After she died and her friends in Joppa called upon Peter to come, they showed him all the clothing that she had made. The story ends happily because the Lord used Peter to raise her up from death.

In my years of working with groups to discover spiritual gifts, I have noticed that the Lord blesses many with this gift—probably because it is foundational to a well-run church.

Teaching

The teacher has a central role in the life of the church because he clarifies truth that God has already revealed. He delights in thinking through and researching the truth of God as it is presented in Scripture, Christian books or sermons. The teacher enjoys accumulating knowledge and loves to communicate that knowledge both to groups and to individuals.

A Spirit-filled teacher is biblically oriented and careful about his use of Scripture, and is usually ready to correct those who abuse Scripture. The teacher needs to be careful that he does not depend upon his own intelligence or his own mastery of knowledge as the source of his ministry. He must depend upon the Holy Spirit's ministry.

The teacher, unfortunately, may have a difficult time maintaining a consistent devotional life; his head often gets in the way of his heart, we might say. He also is vulnerable to pride of the knowledge he has accumulated and his ability to communicate that to others. He also can become bogged down in concentrating on small details of Scripture rather than communicating the basic life principles that will give the greatest help.

Dr. George Cannon, who taught for many years at Nyack College and Bethel Theological Seminary, comes to mind quickly when I think of people who were spiritually gifted as teachers. His interest in the biblical texts took him to research depths and exegetical heights that were very rare. His love for the classroom setting was obvious. Unlike many professors, Professor Cannon did not care about academic reputation or professional accolades. He remained a humble man, which endeared him all the more to his students.

But not all teachers are teachers by profession. My Aunt Florence spent most of her life in Thailand as a missionary. She helped manage a guest home, worked in literature translation, and even provided American meals for the King of Thailand and his family from time to time. These are the ministries that most people knew about. When I first visited Bangkok, I learned that she also translated the New Testament from Greek into Thai, she helped start a Bible College, and she mentored its first president. And whatever she did, she was eager to train others to do what she could do—a sure mark of someone with the gift of teaching.

Exhorting (or Encouraging)

The exhorter encourages and builds others by helping them see the possibility of growth in their own lives. She is eager to encourage the faith of other Christians by recommending steps of action that will promote growth. Literally, *exhort* means to come along side someone to urge him to pursue a course of conduct. Consequently, the exhorter may often have an effective ministry of counseling individuals.

Usually the exhorter is more effective in small group settings and in one-on-one encounters than in large groups. In her counseling ministry, she will not only help people to sense the possibility of growth, but she may also recommend ways of approaching that possibility and hold them accountable for pursuing it.

The exhorter often helps people understand how God is speaking to them through the circumstances of life, including times of discouragement and adversity. She helps them use such experiences to deepen their faith rather than deepen their depression. The exhorter uses Scripture in a very practical way by looking at it topically and showing how its insights relate to the issue at hand in the life of the other person.

The exhorter needs to be careful that she does not become discouraged when the progress of others is slow. She may tend to expect too much too soon in the way of results. She also needs to be careful that she does not become proud when good results are achieved in other people's lives.

As with servers, it seems that the Lord has placed many exhorters in the body of Christ, and this should not surprise us because they are the best disciple makers. Fran Larsen is a prime example of an exhorter. For many years she organized, led and taught a women's Bible study called "All the Women of the Bible." Hundreds of women were discipled through that ministry. After she retired and moved to Hilton Head, South Carolina, she became area director for Community Bible Studies so that she could continue her phenomenal ministry to women. While her teaching was excellent, what made Fran so effective was her buoyant spirit, her attention to every individual woman, and her courage in urging them to apply biblical principles to their lives.

Exhorters have a way of making you feel better about yourself. They believe in you more than you believe in yourself. Chuck Swindoll surely has the effect on people. So does Chuck Smith. So does Charles Stanley. (Maybe it's in the name!) As pastors of large churches, they could easily become bogged down with endless administration, but somehow they seem to transcend their own ministries to touch hundreds of individuals to help them have the confidence to become obedient followers of Christ. I don't know if these three men would say their spiritual gift is exhorting, but they surely fit the profile.

Giving

The giver is deeply motivated to earn and then entrust finances to others for the furtherance of their ministry. He tends to organize his financial interests in order to gain more funds for the work of the Lord. The giver enjoys giving what he has, but he is very careful about how he does it, being concerned about his stewardship—the making of wise investments in the Lord's work.

The true giver does not seek public recognition. He wants to obey the Lord's word about not doing his alms giving in public. He is quite alert to the financial and material needs of others, and his gifts usually are generous and of high quality. He has a concern to feel that he is a part of the ministry to which he contributes.

The giver must be careful not to use his financial resources to manipulate others or to buy their appreciation. He also must be careful not to judge others because they may not seem to be as generous as he is. Often a giver will tend to measure spiritual success by the way the Lord blesses materially. Since wealth is not a stamp of approval, the giver needs to be careful about this.

Certainly, pride is the enemy of this gift as well, so the giver needs to realize that all he has comes from and belongs to the Lord!

When we were considering the manifestation of faith in chapter five, I mentioned the way the Lord used my dad to help finance the beginning of Tele-Mission International by giving $500 he intended to use as down payment for a new car. This was not at all an unusual event in his life as he frequently expressed his gift of giving. Some people considered him to be a workaholic and to be obsessed by the bottom line of his business. What they did not know, however, was that what he was really obsessed about was giving as much money as possible from his profits to missions.

One Christian layman I know owns several service establishments, and he manages them carefully to be highly profitable. He has also set up a foundation into which he deposits some of the earnings so that he can help fund several dozen Christian ministries that he and his wife believe in. He does not consider his generosity to be anything exceptional because he truly believes that all he has belongs to the Lord. I'm sure there are many others whom God has raised up with this kind of heart to fuel many worthy ministries.

Organizing (or Leading)

The sixth gift goes by several different names—organizing, leading, ruling or administrating. The basic motivation is to coordinate the activities of others for the achievement of common goals. We will call this the gift of organizing.

The organizer is often a leader who is able to envision the long-range goals of the group and to organize ministries and efforts toward the accomplishment of those goals. The organizer often has an uncanny ability of knowing the assets that are available to her in personnel and materials, and she is eager to delegate responsibility to those who are trustworthy. She is not necessarily a person who quickly grabs the opportunity to be a leader. She may allow others to do what they can until her gift is needed.

Sometimes the organizer may be seen as harsh and demanding, not sensitive to the limitations of others. She may be more task-oriented than people-oriented. While it is true that she enjoys seeing all the pieces come together, the projects themselves are not really as important to her as the process of getting people involved in working together to achieve an important objective.

The organizer may easily be misunderstood and often must endure negative reaction from those whom she is leading. They may think she carries too much authority, or suspect that her purpose in delegating responsibility is to avoid work herself.

The danger associated with this gift is the misuse of power. The organizer can be proud of her influence over others and may be found to be using people to get to work done rather than "using work to get people done." This is a very important concept. The Lord's type of leadership was always people-oriented rather than task-oriented (see Luke 22:25, 26).

Doris, a member of my first church, was clearly an organizer. She could always see the big picture better than others, and she easily drew others into projects that helped the church make its maximum impact. During a building program it seemed Doris was always around, sort of like an unofficial project manager. She had enough tact and grace not to be in the way of the construction crew, but somehow things just seemed to go more smoothly and extra touches were evident when Doris was present. Once the building was completed, it occurred to the governing board that extra responsibilities would fall on the pastors, possibly distracting them from their primary ministries. It didn't take too long to find the solution—hire Doris, which we did. Thank God for organizers.

Showing Mercy (Empathy)

To empathize means to identify with and comfort those who are in distress. The empathizer is able to relate on an emotional level with people and minister to them in weeping and rejoicing. To have empathy means to feel along with someone. In fact, it is more than feeling sorry for them; it is actually feeling the pain they are experiencing as well.

The empathizer is someone who quickly detects joy or distress in either an individual or a group. He readily gravitates to those who are in distress, desiring to remove the hurts and to bring healing.

It is difficult for the empathizer to be firm, so he often becomes distressed with those who are not as softhearted as he is. This lack of firmness may appear to others as weakness and indecisiveness, as though his emotions guide him, rather than logic or the Word of God.

Since the empathizer is attracted to those in distress, he often will side with the underdog, becoming judgmental about others who may be part of that person's problem. An empathizer needs to be careful that he does not take upon himself the very problem that he is trying to solve in the other person. He needs to be careful that he does not resent others who are not as sensitive as he is.

Again, the problem of pride may creep into this gift, since the empathizer is often someone that other people will open up to quite easily. The empathizer may feel good about being the kind of person he is and even be proud of it.

My mentor Paul Bubna had the gift of mercy. Though he was a powerful preacher, an insightful teacher, and a very good pastor, by his own admission his spiritual gift was mercy. Because he was an introvert, many people did not get to know him well enough to understand how deeply he felt about the needs of people. His goal was never to grow a large church but to care for the needs of people – physical, material, emotional and spiritual needs. Never would he allow a person from his church be in a hospital more than two days before someone from the pastoral staff visited that person. As president of the Christian and Missionary Alliance (only a few years before he died), Paul was the first one to express deep concern for ministering to the minority communities in the denomination. Serving with him on three occasions in my life, I learned that mercy is a very powerful gift. For more inspiration from the life of Paul Bubna, I'd encourage you to read his biography co-authored by Reverend Ron Jones and me.[21]

Ministering Through the Spiritual Gifts

Each spiritual gift is designed and distributed by the Lord to bring blessing to the life of the Church. Below I list the seven gifts again and suggest some specific ways each one may be used by God in the life of the church. These are merely suggestions based on experience and observation. God's Spirit is so creative that we should never try to impose limitations or boundaries on how He will work.

It seems that certain spiritual gifts may more likely be combined with certain manifestations than others, so I will mention the combinations that seem to "travel together." We have no biblical text to verify this, so just receive this idea as conjecture and see if your experiences and observation bear it out. Our purpose is to show the fluidity of the life of the Spirit and how gifts and manifestations may work together, not to build a systematic theology of *pneumatika*.

The Ministering Prophet
- God will use you to guard the reputation of the Church by your keen sensitivity to righteousness.
- You will frequently manifest words of knowledge and discernment of spirits.
- You will not accept compromise and will call people to decision.
- You will be effective as you speak in love.

The Ministering Server
- You will be foundational to the effective functioning of the Church.
- You will frequently manifest helps, hospitality and miracles.
- You will demonstrate the character of Christ by honoring others above yourself.
- Do not become weary in well doing.

The Ministering Teacher
- You will guide many in the Church into enthusiasm and correct understanding of Scripture.
- Words of wisdom, and words of knowledge will be manifest in you.
- You will prevent many from erroneous use of God's word and much spiritual harm.
- Be fervent in spirit as well as intellect.

The Ministering Exhorter
- You will be the Holy Spirit's chief helper in counseling and encouraging God's people.
- Your primary manifestations may be faith and gifts of healing.
- Your hope and trust in God will inspire many to believe in and take steps toward their own growth.
- Be patient and persistent in prayer.

The Ministering Giver
- Your zeal for the prosperity of the work of the Lord will be a blessing to many.

- You will manifest faith and the discernment of spirits.
- Your sense of stewardship and investment will guide the Church.
- You will be cheerful in giving.

The Ministering Organizer
- You will help set the agenda and lead the people into the Church's future.
- You will manifest prophetic insight into God's plans so you can align with them and be given words of wisdom for leading.
- You will not be sidetracked by trends or tempted by shortcuts.
- God's people will expect a lot from you.

The Ministering Empathizer
- You will know God's heart and be His arms and tears for many.
- The manifestations of faith and gifts of healing will work through you.
- People will readily confide in you with secrets they will tell no one else.
- Your pastoral heart may be vulnerable to wounding.

A Gift That Fits

This discussion of spiritual gifts is not intended just to rouse your curiosity. It is a good thing to know your spiritual gift; God will reveal that to you when He chooses to do so. Not knowing your gift, however, will never keep you from ministering. Many godly people have gone throughout their lives serving the Lord faithfully and effectively without being able to say, "I am an exhorter," or "I am a prophet." It is always better to seek the Giver than the gift.

Ultimately, God's concern is not just that we as individuals know our gifts and have joy ministering. We must remember that He is building a temple, and we are parts of that temple. Someone may be a brick, another a window, another a roof tile, another a pillar. There is no glory in any part of the temple. The glory is in the presence of God in the midst of all parts of the temple. We must never isolate ourselves or our spiritual gifts from the body of Christ.

It is God's desire that His glory be seen in us as individuals rightfully taking our places in the body of Christ and ministering effectively in our unique way, but never doing so for selfish reasons. The Lord wants to build a temple, and He has included each of us in His plan. It is far better for each of us to be concerned about fitting in well with His plan than to worry about whether or not anyone else notices what beautiful parts of the temple we are!

CHAPTER SIX:
SEEKING, EXPERIENCING AND KNOWING THE FILLING OF THE HOLY SPIRIT

After years of modernization in industry and technology, society has advanced so far that it seems nothing is beyond possibility. Concepts about travel and communications that a century ago seemed to be fanciful fiction are now reality, and even outdated. But what if sometime in the next decade a dominant world government would emerge and forbid the use of electricity, petroleum and other kinds of fuel? Imagine how our world would come to a screeching halt, as we would be virtually without power.

In a sense, that is what happened in church history over 1500 years ago. The church had been growing dynamically, energized by the Holy Spirit and His gifts. Everyday Christians lived with Pentecostal power, and the world was being turned upside down by the gospel. But then something—success, politics, religion, heresy, materialism, immorality—something pulled the plug of the Spirit, and the power was gone. The world entered the Dark Ages. Even the church was a dark place for centuries. Only a few times and in a few places did it seem that the electricity was turned on.

But within the past century the spiritual electricity has been rediscovered, and all over the world Christians are plugging in to the power of the Holy Spirit. A global revival is occurring, and the Church of Jesus Christ is growing rapidly. Christians are being renewed by the power of the Spirit and finding ways to use their spiritual gifts and to share their faith with others.

Who are these new breeds of spiritually charged believers? Pentecostals? Charismatics? Evangelicals? Catholics? Orthodox? Yes, all of the above. Their religious and denominational labels mean very little, as they are more accurately defined by the presence and power of the Holy Spirit in their lives. Of course, the Holy Spirit has been present in all true believers since Pentecost, but what sets these Christians apart is their confidence in the work of the Spirit in them. And this confidence is borne by the assurance that comes from manifestations of the Spirit as they have been baptized and filled.

Those who have been most open to the reality and empowerment of manifestations of the Spirit are part of the enormous Pentecostal global movement. While many insist that tongues is the only legitimate evidence of the baptism of the Holy Spirit, others do not. What they have in common, however, is their absolute belief that God works miraculously today in and through His people. Modern Pentecostals see a direct continuity from Acts 2 into the present, and they expect God to "show up" when they are ministering. Now in its second century, the modern Pentecostal movement, which began in 1906 under William J. Seymour at an Azusa Street meeting in California, has more than 580 million adherents, and is growing by 19 million per year, or 54,000 per day.[22]

While the world Christian mission is greatly blessed by the Pentecostals and those in the charismatic movement, one does not have to go by one of those labels in order to experience the baptism of the Holy Spirit and to walk in His anointing. But people need to be taught that this experience is available for all Christians, and without it, very little will be accomplished for God.

Today, so many believers pray for the fullness of the Holy Spirit, but do not know to expect or "tarry for" a manifestation that will give them the confidence that they have been filled. We have been taught just to take it by faith, when in Scripture it is clear that as believers tarried in expectancy, God broke through with His manifest presence and worked a dynamic change in each person who was filled.

Unfortunately, this is not merely a theoretical issue. A friend of mine had an interesting experience at a Christian camp. A well-known evangelist was preaching about the fullness of the Holy Spirit. My friend and his wife were newly married and excited about going into pastoral ministry. They responded to the altar call and were praying when the speaker reached them and asked, "What is it you want from God?" They told him they would soon be taking a church and wanted to be sure they were filled with the Holy Spirit. He replied, "Have you asked to be filled?" They answered, "Yes." Then he said, "Well then, you have been filled. Take it by faith." My friend said, "That's it? Now, just go buy a milkshake?" He was assured that just as we take our salvation by faith, so must we take our filling by faith. Years later, my friend sought, tarried and received the baptism of the Holy Spirit with a confirming manifestation.

So, What Does It Mean to Be Filled?

Ephesians 5:18 is a key verse for understanding the filling of the Holy Spirit: *And do not get drunk with wine, for that is dissipation, but be filled with the Spirit.* The preciseness of the Greek word for filling is helpful here. It is in the imperative mood, meaning it is not a proposal or a suggestion but an authoritative command. It is obligatory, not optional. Second, it is plural, meaning the whole Christian community, not an elitist few, is to be filled. Third, it is in the passive voice and rendered correctly by the New English Bible *let the Holy Spirit keep filling you.* There is no technique to learn or formula to recite. It is rather like opening the valve for a gas to be released. And fourth, the word for *be filled* is in the present tense suggesting a continuously needed experience, rendered properly, *be being filled.*

97

Notice that Paul uses the imagery of drinking so that we might get an understanding of what it means to be filled. The imagery suggests several things about the filling of the Holy Spirit.

First we should note that filling is not the same as conversion, regeneration, baptism in the Holy Spirit, or sanctification. Conversion and regeneration are synonymous and are one-time events that are not repeatable.[23] Baptism in (or with) the Holy Spirit is also a one-time event that usually occurs sometime after conversion. It is the initial filling, and it is marked by a manifestation of the Spirit that may not always be present in subsequent fillings. Sanctification is the process of being made more holy.

Being filled with the Holy Spirit, however, is a repeatable event, suggested by the fact that a drinking cup can be emptied and refilled many times. The reason for repeated fillings is that the purpose for being filled with the Holy Spirit is to engage in effective ministry. It is the same idea as anointing in the Old Testament. As we give of ourselves in effective ministry we need repeated fillings for further ministry.

Is it possible to be saved, baptized in the Spirit and filled all at once? Theoretically, yes, this is the ideal situation, but as Dr. George Pardington notes, this would be rare.

> *From ... the experience of the Apostolic Church, as recorded in the book of Acts, we may learn that God is sovereign in His operation, and that doctrinal distinctions made by man cannot shut Him up to set ways of working.*
>
> *Now, in light of these facts we believe that conversion and the reception of the Holy Spirit should go hand in hand, so to speak. That is, while they are distinct experientially, they should not be separated chronologically. But in the lives of few Christians today, comparatively speaking, is this true.... Generally an interval of time--and often it is a long period--does occur. Indeed, some truehearted children of God never seem to know from experience the personal indwelling of the Holy Spirit.... We cannot refrain*

from saying that we believe God never intended that there should be a barren state of Christian experience between regeneration and sanctification, but that conversion should be immediately followed by a life of victory over sin and self in union with the indwelling Christ and through receiving the gift of the Holy Spirit.[24]

Sanctification

In some circles the word *sanctification* is used interchangeably with the filling of the Holy Spirit. But there are some differences between the concepts. Sanctification means to be separated or set apart for a holy purpose. It includes being separated from the world and from sin, and being separated unto God and holiness in life. The word was used in the Old Testament to talk about dedicating a sacrifice or a temple utensil for the glory of God. Sanctification always includes the concept of holiness.

To be sanctified means always to have a burning desire to be right with God. Paul wrote to the Ephesians saying that we should *be holy and blameless* (Ephesians 1:4). He told the Thessalonians that *God has not called us to be impure, but to live a holy life* (1 Thessalonians 4:7). He explained to the Colossians that it is Christ's desire that the believer should be presented *holy in his sight, without blemish and free from accusation* (Colossians 1:22). The will of God is for every believer to be sanctified or made holy.

Perhaps the best-known verse about sanctification is 1 Thessalonians 5:23, *May God himself, the God of peace, sanctify you through and through. May your whole spirit, soul and body be kept blameless at the coming of our Lord Jesus Christ.* This is followed by the glorious promise of verse 24, *The one who calls you is faithful and he will do it.*

Sanctification, like the baptism and filling of the Holy Spirit, is a deeper work of the Holy Spirit, but its focus is more on growth in holiness than on empowerment for service. Truly, however, sanctified believers will likely be baptized and filled, and vice versa.

Paul L. King, D.Min. Th.D., Assistant Professor of Theology, School of LifeLong Education at Oral Roberts University and an ordained minister of The Christian and Missionary Alliance, was kind enough to read an abstract of this book prior to my writing the chapters. Corresponding with one of my colleagues, he wrote:

> *His study on...people just receiving by faith without any Evidences is very interesting, and rings true. Of course, the early Higher Life, Keswick, and Wesleyan holiness movements did stress receiving by faith without seeing immediate evidence, but they expected eventual evidences in greater holiness of life and increased power. The sanctifying baptism in the Spirit in the 19th century could be accompanied by evidences such as holy laughter, trembling, sense of an electrical current, falling under the power, etc., but was not required. (Phoebe Palmer and Hannah Whitall Smith especially taught receiving by faith without expecting thrills and chills). After Azusa Street, Simpson and the Alliance emphasized holy living through the fruit of the Spirit as the chief evidences (increased love, joy, unity, peace, humility, desire for prayer and the Word--if tongues was not accompanied by these, then the tongues experience was suspect.). By the way, Azusa St. catalyst William Seymour eventually recanted evidential tongues and came to this position. He said, "I don't care how many tongues you speak in. If you don't have the fruit of the Spirit, you don't have the baptism in the Spirit." Bosworth, a friend of Seymour, after he came into the Alliance, also stressed receiving by faith, but expected some sort of eventual signs..[25]*

King raises several important points in these few paragraphs.
- Early Alliance people did expect some evidential manifestation of the Spirit to attest to the filling of the Holy Spirit
- Greater holiness and power for effective service for Christ were expected outcomes of a person's baptism in the Spirit
- While esoteric manifestations were not uncommon, many movements, including the Alliance, believed that confirming evidences of the Spirit's fullness were qualities like the fruit of the Spirit.

How Can I Be Filled?

While the focus of this book is not on how to be filled, but on how to know that I am filled, it would be unkind to leave some believers wondering what steps to take to enter into this deep work of God.

Thank God, it is not a complicated procedure! Five words can really express the process of being filled with the Holy Spirit. First, *surrender* to Him. This is what we are doing when we obey the command in Romans 12:1, to present our bodies as a living and holy sacrifice to the Lord. When we surrender our will to God, we become His bond-slave; we are *crucified with Christ* (Galatians 2:20). We not only acknowledge that God has total ownership of us, but we willingly surrender our rights and autonomy.

Second, *ask* to be filled. God is more eager than we are for us to be filled with His Holy Spirit. Jesus said to his disciples, *If you, then, though you are evil, know how to give good gifts to your children, how much more will your Father in heaven give the Holy Spirit to those who ask him!* (Luke 11: 13). As simple as this sounds, many Christians never bother to ask to be filled with the Holy Spirit.

Third, *obey* God. When Peter was testifying to Jewish leaders about the resurrection of Jesus Christ, he said, *We are witnesses of these things, and so is the Holy Spirit, whom God has given to those who obey him* (Acts 5:32). Obedience is always a sign of submission. We cannot expect God to fill us with Himself if we are still filled with ourselves, wanting our way, insisting on our rights, doing our thing. We must be obedient.

Fourth, *believe* Him. The Galatian Christians at one time began to backtrack on their belief. In very strong warnings Paul said, *I would like to learn just one thing from you: Did you receive the Spirit by observing the law, or by believing what you heard?* (Galatians 3:2). Once you have surrendered fully to the Lord, have asked for the Holy Spirit to fill you and have begun to obey him, it is important that you believe what God has said.

Fifth, *anticipate* a manifestation of His infilling. When the almighty, infinite God fills you, wouldn't you think somehow you should notice it? Think of these experiences: jumping into icy water, touching a live electrical wire, eating the most delicious dessert ever made, hitting your thumb with a hammer, cracking the sound barrier in a jet, being frightened out of your wits by a spider, and falling in love with the most wonderful person in the world. What do they have in common? In each case, the dramatic experience brings about a sensation that you cannot help but notice. And these are merely earthly, physical experiences. But they involve our entire being. We may experience bodily sensations like goose bumps or static hair. And we will experience emotions like joy or fear.

Similarly, when you are baptized with the Holy Spirit, God's fullness will produce some kind of manifestation. It may not happen instantly. You may need to tarry, to keep praying and seeking -- to keep believing and expecting. It is the Father's delight and good pleasure for you to have total certainty that He has filled you with Himself. Jesus affirmed that to His earliest followers:

> *Now suppose one of you fathers is asked by his son for a fish; he will not give him a snake instead of a fish, will he? Or if he is asked for an egg, he will not give him a scorpion, will he? If you the, being evil, know how to give good gifts to your children, **how much more shall your heavenly Father give the Holy Spirit to those who ask Him?** Luke 11:11-13*

Laying on of Hands

One further step might be helpful. If you have confidence in the spiritual integrity and authority of a man or woman of God, you might ask him or her to lay hands on you and pray for the baptism and filling of the Holy Spirit. Many people have received this divine blessing by this act of impartation.

We notice frequently in Scripture that the Holy Spirit was imparted by a man of God who laid his hands upon the person who was seeking to be filled with the Holy Spirit. In Acts 8:14-17 Peter and John laid hands upon the Samaritans while they prayed for them to receive the Holy Spirit. In Acts 9:12 the glorified Jesus spoke to Ananias to lay his hands upon Saul (Paul) for him to regain his sight and be filled with the Holy Spirit. In Acts 19:2 Paul laid his hands on the Ephesians, as he prayed for them to receive the Holy Spirit. Paul admonished Timothy *to kindle afresh the gift of God which is in you through the laying on of my hands* (2 Timothy 1:6).

The laying on of hands is used to impart many other wonderful spiritual blessings, including transferring family blessing (Genesis 48:14), setting apart for service (Numbers 8:10, 11; Acts 6:6), appointing a successor (Numbers 27:18-23), imparting blessing to children (Matthew 19:13), healing (Matthew 9:18), and bestowing spiritual gifts (1 Timothy 4:14). We should not hesitate to minister to others or to seek ministry from others in this biblical way.

Now if after going through the steps above, including tarrying for a reasonable period, you do not have evidence of the Spirit's filling, it would be wise to re-examine yourself to make sure there are no unresolved conflicts or hidden agendas or sins that cloud your spirit. If you find something that does interfere with the fellowship between God and you, it may not be enough merely to confess it. God may be expecting you to make it right by some act of restitution or restoration. Once you have a clear channel of communication and fellowship with God, He will be eager to fill you with His presence through the Holy Spirit.

Let me remind you of Dr. A. W. Tozer's quote, cited earlier, although this version is slightly different and from a different source:

> *There are many people in our churches who would like to think that they are filled with the Holy Spirit—even though they don't know it. This is a most shocking thing, and I am sure that this is one of the attitudes through which Satan opposes the doctrine of the genuine Spirit-filled life. And yet, our people don't want to hear too much about it.*

David E. Schroeder

Let me say that I do not find in the Old Testament or in the New Testament, neither in Christian biography, in Church history or in personal Christian testimonies, the experience of any person who was ever filled with Holy Spirit and didn't know it!

I can be dogmatic about this on the basis of deep study: No one was ever filled with the Holy Spirit who didn't know that he had been so filled!

Furthermore, none of the persons in the Bible and none that I can find in Church history or biography was ever filled with the Holy Spirit who didn't know when he was filled. I cannot find that anyone was ever filled gradually.[26]

CHAPTER SEVEN:
EMPOWERED BY THE SPIRIT

Eddie Gibbs, Donald A. McGavran Professor of Church Growth at Fuller Theological Seminary, recommends that in every seminary classroom there should be a co-teacher who is always ready to ask: "So what?"[27] Good theology must be supported by ample evidences of experience that will demonstrate and support the integrity of the teaching. Thus, we conclude this book with a chapter of testimonies.

Personal Testimonies

In the fall of 2004, I emailed 113 people, randomly selected from a much larger list. Twenty-two responded to this email and the seven questions I asked (although not everyone answered every question). This was not intended to be a statistically valid survey. I am not at all interested in the statistics. What I was going for were real life testimonies of individuals and their experiences and relationship with the Holy Spirit. Hence, the group was not as widely representative as would be desired. Six individuals are non-Caucasian, only one is a woman (although nineteen received the survey), and six are not members of the Christian and Missionary Alliance. Twelve are clergy; five are educators; five are laymen. I am grateful to those who responded to this questionnaire:

> *I am writing a book on how a believer in Christ can be sure that he or she has been filled with the Holy Spirit. One chapter will*

be based on testimonies of people who respond to this survey. The survey is for those who have experienced the filling of the Holy Spirit. If you are not aware of such an experience in your life, please disregard [this email].

1. Were you filled with the Holy Spirit as a definite experience subsequent to your conversion?

2. Approximately how long after your conversion experience did you receive this infilling?

3. At the time of your filling or sometime later was there a manifestation of the Holy Spirit that convinced you beyond doubt that the experience was for real? If so, what was that evidence?

4. Of the nine manifestations of the Spirit listed in 1 Corinthians 12: 8-10, which ones have you experienced?

> *Word of wisdom*
> *Word of knowledge*
> *Faith*
> *Gifts of healing*
> *Effecting of miracles*
> *Prophecy*
> *Distinguishing of spirits*
> *Speaking in tongues*
> *Interpretation of tongues*

5. Have you had other manifestations of the Spirit? If so, what were they and how often have you had such experiences?

6. What has been the primary effect of your being filled with the Holy Spirit?

7. If you care to take the time, would you write a few paragraphs telling the story of how you received the filling of the Holy Spirit? Are you willing for me to use your story in the book I am writing? Thank you.

Although nearly all respondents gave permission to reveal their identity, I have chosen not to do so.

Rather than just recording a table of responses, I believe it will be more helpful to note the general direction of responses to the seven questions and to highlight testimonies and exceptions that may be useful in instructing us further and opening us to further inquiry and growth in our life with the Spirit.

Were you filled with the Holy Spirit as a definite experience subsequent to your conversion?

The overwhelming testimony of the respondents was YES. Out of the twenty-two, only three did not give a definitive answer. One wrote, *If you mean an experience that involved an emotional or physical event, no. If, on the other hand you mean a definite spiritual awakening due to teaching, yes.* This person seems to have assurance of being filled with the Holy Spirit, but the answer does not speak to the issue of its timing in relation to conversion, or whether the teaching was one episode or a process. Another exception from the group said, *Not as a single definite experience, but as a process.* In my opinion, this is confusion between the processes of being sanctified in Christian growth and having had a crisis experience of being filled with the Holy Spirit. As Dr. Tozer said in a quote from an earlier chapter, when a person if filled with the Holy Spirit, although he or she may not remember the exact date or time of the experience, the event itself will impress itself vividly in the person's consciousness.

One other exception to the definitive positive responses came from one whose conversion in 1960 was couched in teaching that *taught that every believer is filled with the Holy Spirit. In my journey, I have seen those who live as though they were filled with His Spirit and other Christians who do not display the same level of faith, joy, peace and boldness in their walk.* It is unclear from this response whether the individual was filled with the Holy Spirit subsequent to conversion.

All other nineteen responses were simply *Yes*, or *Yes* with a brief comment. Two of the comments are of interest.

> *My Christian experience can easily be interpreted that way. In other words, yes. I was raised in a CMA Christian home. I'm not*

sure when I became a Christian, but it was likely sometime in my childhood or youth. I experienced the crisis when I was 29.

Yes - It was definitive in that there was a qualitative difference in my heart's confidence in the person and presence of Jesus Christ. I noticed that this led to an increasing impact on my witness for him during my high school years. It was a measurable difference in the eyes of my peers. The filling was so strong that night in church that I found myself worshipping him in tears and great joy. It was an unforgettable experience and I've had subsequent filling but the first was noticeably unique and strong.

The first comment testifies to the common experience of many years lapsing between a childhood experience and the initial filling of the Holy Spirit. The second comment takes up the themes of gaining confidence and entering a qualitatively new dimension of spiritual life and service after a rather dramatic experience with the Holy Spirit.

Approximately how long after your conversion experience did you receive this infilling?

As above, three individuals answered the question with some uncertainty, not just about the timing, but also about the experience itself. One person said, *For me, I have gone "in and out" of periods where I felt the power of the indwelling of the Holy Spirit. Usually, the periods when I don't feel as indwelled is when I neglect my quiet times, make decisions without adequate prayer, etc.* This response is consistent with the person's belief that every believer is filled with the Holy Spirit.

Of the other nineteen, eight received the initial filling of the Holy Spirit three years or less after their conversion. One received the infilling the same day as his conversion, but he was aware of two experiences, and his testimony of the second experience reveals manifestations that generally do not coincide with the conversion experience.

Eleven received the fullness of the Holy Spirit more than three years after conversion, the average time being 14.5 years. Some of these were approximations, but generalizing from this it seems that maybe more than half of the Christians who testify to receiving the filling of the Holy Spirit as a definite act subsequent to conversion live at least a decade before entering into that experience. Here are some of their stories:

- *Approximately 20 years (I accepted Jesus as my Savior at age 13). It was under the teaching of Parris Reidhead that I realized that the Lord Jesus desired that He become not only my Savior, but my Lord. In effect, that He be my all in all.*

- *I call it my crisis experience. It was one year after conversion. It happened when I sensed God calling me to a deeper walk with Him. I tried in my own efforts and failed. When I realized my inadequacy and called out to God for help, releasing all control over my life, then there was a definite filling of the spirit. For days I cried. One day as I was walking, again I sensed a sudden pouring out of the Spirit upon me.*

- *Saved as a very young child; filled with Spirit as a junior at Nyack.*

- *Probably close to 20 years after conversion. I was saved as a young boy in a Christian & Missionary Alliance church, but I never heard about this truth in a way that was understandable and experiential until I was finished with college. Four years of Nyack College in the early 80's did not help me to understand or experience this truth either. I had to go outside the CMA to find the Deeper Life.*

- *It was approximately 6 months after I came to Christ that I came to the altar to receive the filling of the Spirit at a worship service. I still remember the prayer of my heart. The speaker invited us to the front to be filled with the Spirit. I prayed, "Jesus I give you my entire heart. You are my number one and no other. I worship you from the top of my head to the bottom of my feet and I love you."*

At the time of your filling or sometime later was there a manifestation of the Holy Spirit that convinced you beyond doubt that the experience was for real? If so, what was that evidence?

While the next two questions probe further into experiences of **manifestations** of the Holy Spirit, this question does not define that term, nor put any limitations on it. Two people answered this question without further comment, one saying *Yes,* and one saying *No.* The other answers came in four ways.

1.　　Five people answered in terms of **surrendering their lives to the lordship of Jesus Christ**, and its impact on their life of service. Here are a few of those responses:

- *There was no visible manifestation that the Holy Spirit had taken control my life. However, I knew for the first time that if anything of eternal significance was going to be done in and through my life it would because the Spirit of God did it. There was no doubt in my mind that God had taken over the life I then yielded to Him.*

- *Yes, especially under pressure when God has enabled me to submit to what I believe were injustices, especially from other believers.*

- *It was a pretty powerful experience: a compelling urgency to go to the altar (though the speaker's presentation wasn't dramatic); an inner witness as they prayed over me; a continuing sense of elation shared with other seekers for several hours; then a clear persistent conviction of his intention to use me in his service.*

2.　　Another kind of response came from five people who spoke in terms of the manifestation being **the fruit of the Holy Spirit,** mentioned in Galatians 5. Some mentioned only a few of the nine qualities. Here are a few of these testimonies:

- *The Fruit of the Spirit manifested through a sense of peace and joy inherent to all my Christian lifestyle and behavior.*

- *Yes, love, joy, peace, patience, kindness, goodness, faithfulness, gentleness and self-control that were not previously present.*

- *I had a real sense of peace that came over me.*

• *Yes, but the manifestation was not in the physical arena (speaking in tongues, prophesying), rather it has manifested itself in a change of my heart towards others, and a desire to see others saved. He has put a new love in my heart for people – all kinds of people.*

3.   Nine respondents were convinced of their filling by receiving **new power, boldness and/or effectiveness in sharing their faith**. In each case the people seemed be surprised by this newly found ability and courage.

• *Yes, I spoke in tongues and had a stronger sense of conviction, a desire to live holy, and an awareness of power (boldness) for God.*

• *Yes, a supernatural joy manifest by singing and praise and an insatiable desire for God's Word. Also an empowerment to witness with boldness. I was in the Marine Corps and was empowered by the Holy Spirit to share Christ without fear. The transformation in my life by the Holy Spirit's infilling can only be described as supernatural.*

• *Manifestation of Power and Authority in ministry*

• *A deeper passion for God, a total personality change: from a shy reserved person, to a bold woman of God.*

• *Yes there was a manifestation. It was holiness, the ability to overcome temptation in areas of besetting sin. It was also effectiveness in ministry: conversions, exponential growth of the youth group of which I was youth pastor, transformed lives, kids leading kids to Christ without training or prompting, etc. It was revival among the Christian kids and then an awakening and conversions in their peer groups.*

• *There was boldness in me that was uncharacteristic. I was a very quiet and shy person, reserved and I found myself filled with confidence to speak and address spiritual matters to my high school peers and classes. I even chose spiritual topics for my speech class while defending the person and historical credibility of Jesus Christ. My youth leaders noticed that I spoke with a certain level of authority and influence in the youth group even though I was the new kid on the block. I did not ask for this emerging "ministry" it came to me. I didn't want it, that is, speaking boldly to my youth group but I felt so compelled and felt so passionately about spirituals matters.*

4.   A final kind of manifestation mentioned by eight people involved **physical phenomena, a prominent one being the manifestation of speaking in tongues**, which seven of the respondents experienced. Of those seven, four also experienced manifestations in the previous category -- power, boldness, and effectiveness. Here are some of the responses of this group, and I include at the end of this question a lengthy testimony, of a radical encounter with Christ.

•   *Speaking in other tongues, expressions of the charismatic gifts, making of melody in my heart and singing to the Lord, boldness in sharing my faith, deeper communion with God in prayer, etc.*

•   *Yes. Speaking in tongues and a very intense desire for personal holiness.*

•   *Yes—the initial evidence was the love of God poured into my heart in a most obvious and powerful manner. I cried for the first time in many years, and I physically shook from head to toes for hours. I also experienced an amazing empowerment upon my preaching, teaching and ministry. Several months later I began to prophesy & speak in tongues. But the primary effect of my filling was the complete affirmation in my spirit that God was real, alive, active, and deeply in love with me!*

•   *Upon the filling my heart was immediately filled with his divine presence and pleasure. His closeness was evident. I felt arrested under the Presence of the Holy One. I also felt His divine pleasure over me. It was then that I began to lift up my praise to him. It was filled with unusual affection and freedom. I literally felt weight on my shoulders. The love of God was so strong, so very evident. I was awestruck. It was so strong I began to weep. I felt the love of God immensely. My heart was on fire. I can still see the sanctuary and I have only been there twice.*

Soon after this immediate time at the altar of being in His manifest presence I sought to praise him again but this time I found myself speaking in a language I did not understand. I knew very little of the speaking of tongues. I was only a Christian for 6 months and was not raised in the church for the most part. I attended church in the past but it was very, very infrequent. I wasn't afraid but I was intrigued. I had an idea of what was happening and the speaker assured me that everything was OK as he watched a manifestation, not the manifestation, of being filled with the Spirit.

• *Actually I would have to say that the experience itself was in totality a manifestation of the very real presence of the Holy Spirit. At a particular rebellious point in my early teen years, I attended an evening music time at a church in New York. I was interested in spiritual things (including the possible existence of elves, tree nymphs, etc.) and also interested in being a fairly good church person (I was a leader in my youth group - but that required very little spiritual activity on my part, just good organizational skills.) I was wearing my typical shredded blue jeans and old thread bare army jacket, and long hair, etc.*

While sitting in the front row (a bit of that rebellion was pretty evident) waiting for the beginning of the music service, I felt a sudden and somewhat frightening movement of wind or cool air across my face and head. It wasn't exactly air movement, but I felt a change in the "atmosphere" around my body. I looked up a bit startled and saw what later became obviously the leader of the music band coming out of the side door of the church front stage platform. I believe he was coming to make some final adjustments on instruments before the service began. But as he came through the door he had a similar startled and quizzical look on his face and fixed his eyes straight on me across the other side of the sanctuary in the front row. We locked eyes for a moment and somehow, knowingly felt something pretty unusual was going on. No remarks

113

or gestures were exchanged. He left the stage from the same door, looked once over his shoulder and then closed the door.

I was extremely alert and shaking a bit not sure why I was feeling intermittently frightened and excited. As the band came out they began to introduce themselves and play their first songs. I was struck on a very objective level at how interesting it was to see a folk-rock band in a church. In those days I was very enthralled with rock music and frequently attended big concerts with the popular groups - Led Zepplin, the Who, Grand Funk Railroad, Ten Years After, Mountain, - you get the point. I was used to the most innovative church music at being the popular gospel trios and quartets on the Bible Belt circuit. There was very little to catch my attention in those days. But here was a pretty good folk-rock bank in a church. Fascinating

At the same time this objective observation was going on my sense of fear and the overall odd physical/mental/spiritual feeling around me was growing rather intense. At some point during one of the songs (by now I had utterly lost track of what was going on with the songs in the sanctuary and the event) I completely lost my vision. Rather, it's a bit hard to explain; my vision was completely filled up with bright white milky light. I became terrified. I pinched both my arms really hard (fingernail marks the next morning) rubbed and scratched my eyes and truly began to shake. I was told later that at this point or somewhere close to this point I had ended up on the floor in the center aisle. But I was completely unaware of that at the time.

The rest is a bit hard to explain. I heard the Lord Jesus speaking to me. It's so hard to explain how it was both a very crystal clear voice and yet not coming in through my ears, but rather through every part of my being. He said, "Why do you hate me?" And I remember replying, "I don't hate you!" And over and over again He repeated the same phrase to me, "Why do you hate me?" After this repeated several times, I finally, weeping, (again I think it was inwardly - I'm not aware of what I was doing outwardly) cried out

"I do hate You, I'm so sorry, I'm so sorry." It wasn't a conscience realization that was a reflection on data or experiences or things I had done. It was a visceral response. And He spoke back so clearly, "I love you, why do you hate Me?" This dialog was repeated several times until finally I said, "I love you too!" And one last time I heard very clearly from Him, "I love you!"

My sight returned. I was lying propped on my elbow in the aisle of a Baptist Church. I jumped to my feet and ran down the aisle, "It's all real! It's for real! He's alive! Jesus is really real! You can talk to Him! He talks to you!"

I ran out the back of the church and down into the streets of the town shouting, jumping, and saying very much the same thing for the next twenty minutes. I don't advocate this as a method for evangelism. But I really can't be held responsible for what was happening inside me! I ran into a pizzeria and tried to explain to the fellow tossing the dough that Jesus Christ was alive and real and He could talk to Him right then and there. He ought to put down his dough and talk to God. It would change his life forever. He kept flipping the pizza. I ran out and finally made my way back up to the church completely exhausted.

There is much, much more to the story. Others began to experience the presence of the Holy Spirit in powerful ways around the same time. A man, who is now a C&MA pastor but was just a youth back then, had similar experiences, only God visited him during a time of healing. That summer we saw many come to Christ. We saw miracles. We saw changed lives.

Sorry for the long story, but you can imagine that when you ask if there was a manifestation of the Holy Spirit at that time that convinced me beyond a doubt that the experience was for real - the answer is yes.

As fascinating as this story is, as well as the other testimony, the key point not to be lost is the confidence and assurance that the individuals gained by experiencing one or more manifestations of God's Spirit, evidenced in various ways.

As suggested earlier, God is free to manifest himself in any way he chooses. I was interested, however, in learning what individuals experienced in terms of the nine manifestations Paul listed in his first letter to the Corinthians. So, the fourth question of my survey was:

Of the nine manifestations of the Spirit listed in 1 Corinthians 12: 8-10, which ones have you experienced?

- *Word of wisdom*
- *Word of knowledge*
- *Faith*
- *Gifts of healing*
- *Effecting of miracles*
- *Prophecy*
- *Distinguishing of spirits*
- *Speaking in tongues*
- *Interpretation of tongues*

Twenty-one of the twenty-two respondents claim to having experienced anywhere from one to all nine of the manifestations listed in 1 Corinthians 12:8-10. Five of the individuals did not seem to be entirely comfortable with the question, as stated. One person seemed to prefer discussing the gifts found in Romans 12, saying:

> *At times people have said to me, " I recall you saying such and such to me 15 years ago, or two years ago and I never forgot it". Is that the gift of wisdom, or a word of knowledge – I don't know. In Romans 12 Paul discusses what has become known as the gifts of service. I believe I have received the gifts of teaching, administration and exhortation.*

Others qualified their responses by these comments:

Prophecy, if by prophecy you mean forth telling the Word. I don't accept the contemporary Pentecostal definitions of those gifts. In a Word based definition God has given me wisdom, knowledge, faith, healing, miracles, prophecy and discernment, all at different times and places.

Faith- Only one real time where I absolutely knew what I was praying for would come true.

Word of wisdom – Yes, when others say that my words were from God. Faith – Not sure, I have no doubts about my relationship with God. Gifts of healing – I have often prayed for others to be healed; some were.

Four individuals reported only one manifestation. They were:
- *Prophecy (understanding it to mean preaching)*
- *Distinguishing of spirits*
- *Wisdom (or knowledge -- not sure)*
- *Word of wisdom*

Three people had received two manifestations. They came in these pairs:
- *Wisdom and prophecy*
- *Speaking in tongues and interpretation of tongues*
- *Word of wisdom and faith*

Five responded with triplets of manifestations:
- Word of wisdom, word of knowledge, and faith
- Word of knowledge, prophecy, and speaking in tongues
- Faith, distinguishing of spirits, and speaking in tongues
- Word of knowledge, distinguishing of spirits, and speaking in tongues
- Word of wisdom, gifts of healing, and prophecy

Two individuals said they had experienced eight of the nine, the exception being in both cases: interpretation of tongues.

Three people have experienced all nine of these manifestations. Their comments about this are:

- *All nine at various times in my life.*

- *All of them. Not all to the same degree or frequency, but I believe the Holy Spirit is the owner and producer of these manifestations. Therefore, my view is that every believer may experience any or all of them.*

- *At one time or another in the past 30 years - each one of them.*

Truly, these responses are testimony to the truth of 1 Corinthians 12:11:

> *But one and the same Spirit works all these things, distributing to each one individually just as He wills.*

One very interesting observation is that in none of the responses was there a hint of dissatisfaction. The only comment, possibly indicating a desire for more, came from one who said about speaking in tongues, "Not yet." I would suggest that this satisfaction is due, not to a lack of spiritual hunger, but rather, because of having received one or more manifestations, these believers have a sense of confidence that they have been filled with the Holy Spirit. And that is one of the important functions of the manifestations -- to give confidence and assurance to the believer that the Holy Spirit will work through him or her.

As indicated earlier, it is doubtful that the list of manifestations in 1 Corinthians is the totality of ways the Holy Spirit manifests the presence and power of God the Father and Jesus Christ. That is why I asked as the fifth question:

Have you had other manifestations of the Spirit? If so, what were they and how often have you had such experiences?

Three people said, No; three did not respond to the question, and two said No, but with comments, reported here:

- *Again, if you are referring to physical manifestations, no. But I recall Ezekiel's promise, "A new heart I will also give you, and a new spirit will I put within you...." He has done that within me. I love people more; I hate sin more; I want to minister reconciliation; I hurt for the unsaved (but not as much as I should); the sky is bluer; the rose more red; the mountains more majestic; the clouds more thrilling; the bird on wing more astounding; the love for my wife more precious. I stand in awe at a Savior who in spite of knowing all about me, warts and all, chose me and died for me. I can't get over the Grace He pours out on my life day after, day after day. Truly, "goodness and mercy follow me".*

- *If you mean the dramatic manifestations, no. If you mean a consistent testimony to my spirit from the Holy Spirit, a confirmation of His presence in my life, yes.*

Rather than categorizing the other responses or commenting on them, here's what various individuals have said:

- *I have been blessed throughout my ministry with prophetic words that have come to confirm things that God was planning to do to advance His Kingdom in New York City. These words have been a great source of encouragement through the process of the death of a vision.*

- *I often experience heat in my hands when praying for anointing or healing on others. I have also had heat sensations in my body when God has released healing to me.*

- *I have had numerous encounters with the Holy Spirit through dreams and visions.*

- *Power for service.*

- *Visions (quite often).*

- *The gifts of leadership and encouragement seem to also often be present.*
- *An evident manifestation of other gifts as for example: Gifts of Leadership, Teaching.*

- *I have had physical manifestations, including jerking and shaking on several occasions.*

- *Periodically I am moved to tears in ways that make me sense I am "in touch" with the Spirit.*

- *Holy Laughter; shaking and or jerking induced by the presence and power of the Spirit; birth pains in intercession; Spiritual drunkenness.*

- *A gift of leadership (cf. Judges 6:34) -- pretty much a surprise to this introvert. A gift of some specific skills (cf. Exodus 31:3) for specific needs.*

- *I'm not sure where to categorize these, but I have had many occasions where I felt God was telling me the next thing that should happen in the course of a worship service. It wasn't so much a word of knowledge as it was a synchronizing of my spirit with those who were leading worship to where I have several times leaned over and whispered what the next song would be or that we should stop and pray for such and such a person - only to find moments later or minutes later that that's exactly what we did. I have been on the other end of that as well. Twice I have been in the middle of a sermon, stopped and decided we needed to share a song--only to find that someone had already written on a card and asked an usher to pass to me a note saying they felt the Holy Spirit wanted us to sing a song - the exact same song.*

I also think there have been manifestations of the Holy Spirit in community. Times when worship, communion, or community service has exploded on a group of believers in a way that in itself was so powerful and memorable that it actually changed peoples lives.

• *I have had dreams that were very clearly from the Lord. I record such occurrences in order to weigh them against the scriptures and seek the Lord for interpretation and appropriate application.*

Several observations based on these experiences might be useful. In most cases it is quite evident that the manifestation had a positive impact either in ministry or worship. In some cases the Lord ministered to or through the subconscious, as in dreams and visions. Such manifestations occurred frequently in Scripture. For example, in the infancy narratives of Matthew and Luke, Joseph was visited by the Lord or an angel three times with messages: Matthew 1:20; 2:13 and 19. Similarly, the Lord warned the magi in a dream. The Lord sent the angel Gabriel to Zacharias and to Mary in Luke 1:11, 19 and 26. These were visions, not dreams.

Can or does God speak in dreams and visions today? Of course he can. Why not? Does he? Certainly the messages will not likely be history making as much as those in the infancy narratives, but many people believe God has spoken to them, or guided them, by such manifestations. In every case, it is important to weigh everything against scripture and submit any extra-biblical insights to trusted, mature believers for verification.

What about such odd things as laughter, tears, intercessory birth pains, shaking and jerking? These are not in the Bible--does that render them invalid? Skeptics are probably those whose worship is only or mainly a rational experience. Those who have allowed their emotions to respond to God will quite likely have some of these experiences, and therefore, have greater tolerance for the variety of manifestations in worship. Certainly the picture we get of heavenly worship in Revelation is not strictly a cerebral exercise.

It is interesting that the person who said No to the question about having received any of the nine manifestations in First Corinthians has sensed power for service as a continuing manifestation.

The comment above about the Holy Spirit manifesting himself in the context of a community of worshipers should not be missed. In Acts, most of the times when the Holy Spirit falls, it is upon a group of believers.

Some of the respondents seem to consider spiritual gifts and manifestations of the Spirit to be the same thing. Thus, several referred to a gift of leadership or teaching. My hope is that they and others who do not grasp the nuance in scripture might carefully consider the words of the biblical texts so that they do not miss out on manifestations of the Spirit, thinking they have it all because they know their spiritual gift.

What has been the primary effect of your being filled with the Holy Spirit?

The responses to this question surprised me a bit. I had expected a great variety of effects, but found only about four, expressed in different ways.

1. By far the most dominant primary effect has been a **passion to know and please God.** Here are some of the testimonies:

• *A hunger for God...An overriding desire to please God because of His great love for me.*

• *An unquenchable passion for God and God alone, a love for him which goes beyond reason, a driving need to be in His presence, a longing to always know He is pleased with me, I desire to please Him first irregardless of what anyone says of, thinks about or does to me. I lost the fear of man!*

• *...pursuing a deeper relationship with Him has kept me in the "fear of the Lord".*

- *Repeatedly and regularly drawn to God—even after severe and prolonged desert experiences/troubles.*

- *A wonderful sense of His presence.*

2. **A new intimacy with Jesus and a deep desire to be like him:**

- *Becoming more Christ-like.*

- *Empowered life change to daily move toward the image of Jesus.*

- *...just a very intimate and passionate and highly personal friendship/love/awed relationship with Jesus. I was taught that we should pray to the Father "in the Holy Spirit", in the name of Jesus. But I must admit I find myself talking to Jesus all the time like He was just my Best Friend. This is especially true after times of such "filling".*

- *...the motivation, captivation and personally activation from within me to know Jesus Christ and make him known in my life.*

3. **A hunger for holiness and God's Word, and increased sensitivity to sin:**

- *I want to walk in the Spirit and not the flesh – to reckon my body dead unto sin, and alive unto God. I want to know more of the Word, and to see it work out in my daily life.*

- *Deeds and thoughts that I may have overlooked in the past as sin, I now call them by their proper name – sin -- repent and receive forgiveness. I look back and spot presumptuous sins that I know displeased the Lord – and ask forgiveness.*

- *A deeper and continuing understanding of my need for holiness; an insatiable desire to be filled continually. I pray daily for the infilling of the Holy Spirit.*

• *Holiness dramatically and progressively, and anointed effective ministry.*

4. **A new understanding of one's role and new effectiveness in ministry, as well as a strong desire to serve other people:**

• *Fruitfulness in ministry*

• *Greater boldness in living the Christian life and sharing it with others.*

• *A strong sense that God has called me for a specific role and that I should trust Him rather than worry about the future.*

• *A ministry vocation-a clear sense like Jeremiah that the Lord had been preparing me all my life, and that now it was time to work toward that.*

• *A tremendous refocus on others. It seems that in the times when I drift away from such experiences, I become consumed with program, systems, and "getting church right". During the times of most powerful filling and experience with the Holy Spirit there just seems to be an automatic and passionate desire to give, love, serve, and live for the benefit of other people.*

• *Boldness. At the times of closet encounter with the Holy Spirit the idea of being fearful of other peoples' opinion of me, fearful of failure, fearful of looking "weird", just passes away. There is too much going on inside to think about those things. As those moments subside, I'm more prone to be timid and thinking about all the multiple possible errors I might perform.*

• *I want to finish strong for the Lord. To serve my generation, as it was said of David. I'm grateful for salvation and the promise of eternal life, but Salvation has also given me a joy-filled, and fulfilling life, now. I have less prejudice and judging of others. I now see others not just as abstract human beings taking up space on this earth, but children created by God, and for whom Jesus died. I know that Jesus loves them just as much as He loves me, and as God grants me opportunity, to speak to them of Christ's love.*

A final question in the survey elicited some interesting biographical material that should encourage all seekers.

If you care to take the time, would you write a few paragraphs telling the story of how you received the filling of the Holy Spirit?

Parts of some of the stories are recorded in some of the questions above, so I will report from only eleven here:

• *I was a new pastor. Overwhelmed with the task before me. I lay on the floor of my office weeping before God. He met with His Spirit and it has been a journey of repeated fillings since that time.*

• *While serving as a pastor, after about two years of what I considered helpful ministry and involvement in the lives of the congregation, I came to the point of realizing that much of what I had been doing was based upon my own training and preparation and personality. I wasn't satisfied with that. I asked a couple in the church who owned a cottage at Lake Chelan (Washington) if I could use that facility. I went there by myself, immersed myself in the Scripture and prayer. I read V. Raymond Edman's book,* They Found the Secret. *It contains an account of twenty individuals whose lives were effective in ministry. I was struck by these words in the introduction: Out of discouragement and defeat they have come into victory. Out of weakness and weariness they have been made strong. Out of ineffectiveness and apparent uselessness they have become efficient and enthusiastic. The pattern seems to be: self-centeredness, self-effort, increasing inner dissatisfaction and outer discouragement, a temptation to give it all up because there is no better way, and then finding the Spirit of God to be their strength, their guide, their confidence and companion -- in a word, their life. The crisis of deeper life is the key that unlocks the secret of their transformation. It is the beginning of the exchanged life. What is the exchanged life? Really, it is not some thing, it is some One. It is the indwelling of the Lord Jesus Christ made real and rewarding by the Holy Spirit. It is new life for old. It is rejoicing for weariness, and radiance for dreariness. It is strength for weakness, and steadiness for uncertainty. It is triumph even through tears, and tenderness of heart instead of touchiness. It is lowliness of spirit instead of self-exaltation, and loveliness of life because of the presence of the altogether Lovely One. Adjectives can be multiplied to describe it; abundant, overflowing, overcoming, all-pervading, satisfying, joyous, victorious; and each is but one aspect of a life that can be experienced but not fully explained. That was and continues to be my experience.*

• *I was twenty years old. I was stationed at the Marine Corps Air Station in Kaneohe on Oahu. Though I had received Jesus as my Savior at age 8, I found my journey to adulthood spiritually marked by numerous rededications in an attempt to live more Christ like. I had a heart sensitive to the Holy Spirit, but found my rededications somewhat short lived. While in the Marines, the youth sponsor I had while in high school, was killed in a car accident and his wife was in a coma for a couple of weeks. That news got my attention as I thought about their selfless and joyful lives, and their strong commitment to Jesus. God used that accident to bring me to a point of crisis. I was tired of being a carnal Christian that was living in the flesh. I came to a point of complete surrender to the Lordship of Christ, and submitted all I was and had to Jesus. I signed on the bottom line and told Him, whatever He wanted me to be, do or go, He called the shots and I would follow whole heartedly. I was in my car as the Lord and I talked. He knew I needed an experience with Him that would be a watershed time in my life. As I cried out to Him, He met me in an unbelievable way. He filled my car and my life with his joy and peace. He filled my heart with song and praise that I sang at the top of my lungs. He infilled me with boldness to witness. When I arrived on base I shared how God had met me with the corporal of guard on duty. That was the beginning of fearless witness. I also began to have an appetite for the Word of God I had never had. It was the beginning of a whole new life.*

• *As a student at Nyack, I met a number of ex-hippies (Jesus freaks) who were filled with the Spirit. I was attracted to the work of God in their lives and to their zeal and started hanging out with them. One became my girlfriend (and eventually my wife). But it was my brother's influence that triggered my search for the filling of the Spirit. He had become filled with the spirit as a freshman at Houghton, not as a result of anyone at Houghton, but as a result of attending Assemblies of God church. Intrigued, I went with him to that church and was filled with Spirit, receiving the gift of speaking in tongues. As a junior and senior at Nyack and for several years after graduation, I regularly met with a group who prayed in tongues.*

• *I was a freshman student at Houghton. I felt very inadequate in my Christian life. The passage of scripture that spoke to me during this time was Matthew 11:28-30, Come to me, all you who are weary and burdened, and I will give you rest. Take my yoke upon you and learn from me, for I am gentle and humble in heart, and you will find rest for your souls. For my yoke is easy and my burden is light. I joined a special prayer group with 3 or 4 friends in which we simply sought God. During the prayer time I sensed a filling of God's Holy Spirit and a peace from the burdens that I had been carrying. I have always sensed this as the time when God filled me with his Spirit for the first time.*

• *I asked how I could become a Christian and did so. That same night I was prayed over to be filled with the Spirit. Through that night I prayed and at some point began praying in tongues. My life was clearly changed as I desired personal holiness and wanted to share my faith with everyone.*

• *I was led to Lord and accepted Jesus as Savior one month before my first filling, which I now identify as my crisis experience. Before this encounter I was still feeling some of the same urges that I had before conversion. The reason for my hospitalization was an accidental overdose of alcohol and drugs. I was an alcoholic and a severe drug abuser. After my conversion, I was being discipled while still in the hospital by several born-again believers, but I was not completely sure of what had changed in my life after I accepted Jesus as Savior. I had a sense of confidence and assurance of my salvation, but I did not sense a radical departure from a desire to sin, as evidenced by urges to smoke. One morning, while praying in my hospital room, I sensed a strange and intense warmth come over my whole body. This radical warmth startled me, because it had been fairly cold in the room. I lifted my arms up into the air, and I could feel the cold air from my elbows up, but below my elbows it was still intensely warm and good feeling. I pulled my arms down, because I thought I might be having an emotional reaction because of my praying. But I put my arms up again, and again I felt the cold air above my elbows. I continued to do this test several times, until suddenly the warmth entered into my body, and it was no longer around me but inside of me too. A flood of tears came from my eyes and soon after wailing came out of my mouth as I felt that God had touched me in a wonderful new way. My roommate in the bed behind the curtain, yelled out to see if I was okay, and, through my tears, and not sure of what I was saying, I replied, "I have just met the Holy Spirit of God." At that moment I made a covenant with God to never be involved in any sinful activity, especially those that had put me in the state that I was in before I accepted Christ: alcohol, drugs, cigarette smoking, womanizing, cursing, etc. I was instantly delivered from all of these things. Now, almost ten years later I continue to have wonderful experiences with the Holy Spirit, and my walk with Him through Bible study, intimate prayer (including occasionally praying in tongues), and fellowship have increased ever since that day He met me in that hospital room.*

• *In 1987, after several months in ministry, I was exhausted and burning out. At a non-Alliance conference the leader invited pastors to come forward for filling and refreshing. The man that prayed for me asked me if I was ready to receive the Love of the Father. Through my tears I said "yes." At that moment it was as if the top of my head was pulled open and the love of God began to fill me. I had never experienced anything as spiritually real as this in my life. God filled me with His Holy Spirit and sealed me with His love. I have never been the same since.*

• *Raised in a Christian home (CMA) I became a Christian, I am not sure when. I decided to go into the ministry as a vocation. I didn't know how to deal with temptation and sin in my life so I developed a hypocritical lifestyle. I was a Christian and pastor on the one hand in public, and a slave to besetting sin in my mind and heart; I put on the show. Then God interrupted my charade with a health crisis (cancer) and I confessed my sin and inability to Him. He filled me with His Spirit and showed me he could empower me to resist temptation and be holy, not perfectly, but definitely and progressively. I was transformed. No longer was I a slave to sin. I still did and do sin, but there is no sin that is master over me like it used to be. There is no sin the Spirit cannot overcome in me and He does. Further, God began to use me in ministry to transform others. I saw people converted, discipled, called to ministry, and come into transformed living. I saw His church built.*

• *It was at Nyack College during a spiritual emphasis week. I had been reading Tozer's book on the Holy Spirit and the speaker was challenging us in this area. For a week I wrestled with yielding my entire being to another spiritual entity. Finally I knelt by my bed and gave all of me, a full yielding to Jesus Christ and asked Him to fill me with His blessed spirit. There was no emotional supercharge, no manifestation but I knew for a certainty that I was no longer on the throne of my life, that I had the actual presence of God making His abode within me! I am still amazed with this fact and relish it that the Creator of the universe lives within me.*

• *At the age of twelve I was praying at the altar when a sister of the church (pastor's wife) placed her hands on me and began to tell me to ask God for the gift of the Holy Spirit with evidence of speaking in tongues. As I prayed, I experienced a "different" sensation and began to speak with other tongues. Although I was conscious and aware of where I was, I also had a greater sense of God's presence I me and in the church, which is a Spanish-speaking Assemblies of God congregation.*

Do testimonies like these make you hungry for more of God? Are you longing to be filled with the Holy Spirit, if you have not already received the Spirit in this way? Sometimes, just hearing what God has done in others increases our faith to believe, as the old gospel song says, *"what*

He's done for others, He'll do for you." If your heart is crying, "More, Lord; I want the fullness," I suggest you go back to Chapter Four and pray your way through the section called "How Can I Be Filled." The five key words there are Surrender, Ask, Obey, Believe and Anticipate. And if need be, tarry. Don't get discouraged if a manifestation does not come immediately. Persist in seeking. God wants you to be a Spirit-filled Christian more than you can possibly want it. That's why He created you!

So, in the words of Ephesians 5:18, *be being filled with the Spirit.* Ask and receive Him in His fullness. Expect His presence to be manifested in, to and through you. Possibly, ask a godly, Spirit-filled believer to lay hands on you to impart the Spirit's fullness. And may you from this day forward confidently walk in your anointing.

Appendix A:
The Alliance and the Pentecostal Movement

The impact of the founder of the Christian and Missionary Alliance upon the larger body of Christ in the early part of the twentieth century was of enormous proportions. Colleagues of A. B. Simpson, whom he had mentored in the deeper things of God, became founders in their own right of denominations, churches, missions and parachurch ministries in North America and around the world. Hardly could the Presbyterian drop-out pastor have known in November of 1881, when after only two years he left the security of the prestigious Thirteenth Street Presbyterian Church in New York City to become "Christ's freeman," that several global ministries would be spawned from his small beginnings with seven people meeting in the Caledonian (Dance) Hall.

It would be virtually impossible to chronicle the millions of spiritual decisions that go back to the spirit and faithfulness of Albert Benjamin Simpson. He was so many things—modern apostle, pastor, teacher, evangelist, administrator, prophet, missionary statesman, healer, revivalist, author, publisher, businessman, college president, poet, hymnist—but preeminently Dr. Simpson was a spiritual pioneer. He rode the range of America's spiritual frontier, forging new pathways, or rather, recovering long-ago abandoned trails of the spirit that led thousands into lives of deeper consecration and more fruitful service to Christ.

One example of this is the little-known fact that the Assemblies of God denomination had its roots in Simpson's Alliance. To this day, several of the buildings at the AOG Bible college in Springfield, MO, are named for men who were colleagues of Dr. Simpson, prior to the advent of the Assemblies in 1914. The April 2006 edition of *Christianity Today* shows a timeline of significant events in the life of Pentecostalism, beginning with "1887 – Christian and Missionary Alliance founded by A. B. Simpson to promote the 'fourfold gospel." Numerous books have been written to expound on Simpson's influence in the early days of the modern Pentecostal movement.

Writings That Address This Topic

While his life and ministry have been chronicled by several able Alliance writers—notably A. E. Thompson,[28] A. W. Tozer,[29] Robert K. Nicklaus, John S. Sawin and Samuel J. Stoesz,[30] Daniel J. Evearitt,[31] *et. al.,* the picture is amplified greatly by other Simpson scholars and admirers. Of Charles Nienkirchen's book, *A. B. Simpson and the Pentecostal Movement,*[32] Edith Blumhofer, Project Director of the Institute of the Study of American Evangelicalism in Wheaton, said:

> *Simpson has long deserved an in-depth study. A pivotal turn-of-the-century figure, who never found full acceptance in any wing of American evangelicalism, this prolific Canadian nonetheless profoundly influenced popular evangelicalism and Anglo-American Protestantism. Nienkirchen makes careful use of long-unused primary sources to illuminate Simpson's relationships to early Pentecostalism. The result is a suggestive work that offers perceptive insights into early Pentecostalism and the context from which it emerged.*[33]

Not quite as focused on Simpson, but very informative are a few chapters from Carl Brumback's *A Sound From Heaven.*[34] Useful also is an article called *Pentecostal Awakenings at Nyack* by Gary B. McGee, who at the time of writing was associate professor on the faculty of the Assemblies of God Graduate School in Springfield, MO.[35] Some of these works have outstanding bibliographies.

The first two decades of Simpson's new missionary, deeper-life, and social concern ministries saw infantile and adolescent growth with all the excitement, enthusiasm and surprises natural to that time of life. The merged Christian Alliance and Evangelical Missionary Alliance were prospering at home and abroad, fueled by the passion of Simpson's Christ-centered "fourfold gospel."

Dr. Simpson truly did not fit into anyone's mold. Having a strictly reformed theological background and education, he became known as one of the holiness revivalists. Eschatologically dispensational, he contradicted that theology's rejection of spiritual gifts. Though espousing the fundamentals of the faith and vehemently championing that side of the fundamentalist/liberal controversy, he nonetheless outshone the liberals as a social reformer. Though appreciative of earlier missionary movements, Simpson insisted on the indigenous principle from the get-go. And so on; the paradoxes of his life defied labeling.

One of the huge influences in A. B. Simpson's spiritual journey was William E. Boardman's book, *The Higher Christian Life* (1858). Serendipitously discovering this "old, musty book" in his library in 1874, Simpson's eyes were opened to a Jesus-centered worldview from which he developed his fourfold gospel. Not so gradually, Simpson began moving from his Presbyterian, reformed theology to a more Wesleyan holiness perspective. Nienkirchen cites fourteen themes developed in Boardman's writing that captured Simpson's heart and began to appear in his sermons and writings. One of them was "a hermeneutical appeal to the life of Christ, the book of Acts, and Old Testament historical metaphors as biblical support for the doctrine of a Spirit baptism or 'second conversion subsequent to initial regeneration and Spirit baptism.'"[36]

Pioneering in the Spirit, Simpson was truly a forerunner of the Pentecostal movement. Nienkirchen quotes Edith Blumhofer, who said Simpson "vigorously proclaimed in evangelical settings" elements of the Pentecostal message "long before the rise of Pentecostalism."[37] In his own spiritual development Dr. Simpson was not averse to expecting his experience to ratify his understanding of Scriptural teachings, and at times it was evident that his personal experiences opened up new vistas of biblical understanding. For example, his dramatic healing experience at Old Orchard, Maine in 1881, which delivered him from chronic heart disorder, opened his understanding to what became the third part of the fourfold gospel, Christ as Healer.

Without any question, Simpson was more than open—he was definitely a seeker of the fullness of God, and in the early days of the Pentecostal movement he truly seemed baffled that others were so blessed by the manifestation of tongues while he was not. One wonders whether he and the Alliance would have been the frontrunners in the Pentecostal movement had he received that manifestation. Eventually, Simpson took the position that it was a serious shortcoming to seek the (any) gift rather than the Giver, as penned in his famous poem/hymn *Himself.* As we will note later, apparently Simpson never closed down the possibility that God would continue giving new spiritual manifestations to him. Nienkirchen alludes to Simpson's Caleb-like spirit even in old age by calling him a "Seeking Founder of a Seek-not Denomination."

Pentecostal Stirrings At Nyack

By His own sovereign choice near the beginning of the twentieth century God began revival stirrings, first noticed in Wales under the ministry of Evans Roberts. The Wind of God blew west before long and soon there were Pentecostal stirrings and manifestations occurring on the campus of the Missionary Training Institute at Nyack. Brumback quotes from a sermon by Herbert Cox delivered at the Stone Church in Chicago and later reported in the October, 1919 *Latter Rain Evangel:*

> *I remember a revival that broke forth in Nyack. For three weeks preachers, teachers and students were lying upon their faces…. Awful confessions were made…It began at twelve o'clock noon and went on until the next morning. God had struck with mighty conviction. Some tried to get away because they didn't want to confess, but they had to come back and go through with it. I declare unto you that, when the confessions were over, the mighty presence of God filled the place. We walked on tiptoe, the atmosphere was so holy. We were afraid to hear the sound of our own heels in that school…. If you ever heard thunder rolls of intercession, they went forth from that school. You could have heard that body of students a mile away. They prayed as one man, and everybody as loudly as possible, but you knew that God was behind those prayers. I believe that these prayers found their answer in the Pentecostal revival we are in today, for it was just about three months before the Spirit was poured out in Los Angeles.*[38]

This event, if Cox's reporting is accurate and it occurred before the outpouring at Azusa Street, must have occurred in the spring of 1906. However, we must question the timing, as Gary B. McGee notes that at the 1907 General Council of the Alliance, held on the Nyack campus, Professor W. C. Stevens reported that the Holy Spirit…

> *…came suddenly one Sunday noon at the missionary prayer meeting. He wrought sufficiently pungent conviction of sin, beginning with some of the most earnest and consecrated of students, to lead to confession in public of a manner before unknown among us. The meeting continued from noon until suppertime in that line. Sunday evening service began as usual at 7:30 o'clock and soon ran into the same current and did not close until six o'clock the next morning. The eight o'clock chapel service ran on and superseded regular class and study time, not closing until noon. For three weeks this suspension of school work continued, three protracted meetings daily taking the place, and that without human leadership. There was a searching out of sin, its open confession and full judgment, a burning of sin out of heart and life, a melting, leveling, unifying such as we had never known, while transforming effects have since appeared in a gratifying degree. There was resistance in some quarters and probably the Spirit went as far as He thought it was best under all circumstances. It became evident that regular order was to be renewed, which was done in full accord. Many had felt great expectation of a climax of demonstration of enduement, which, however, has not yet come to us. No one pretends to understand all sides of this visitation, its nature, purposes, and limitations; but it can never be forgotten, its effects have never ceased, its culmination may still be coming on.*[39]

George N. Eldridge, chairman of the Committee on Home Work, reported at the 1907 Council, "There is bursting out in many centers a revival which is surely a visitation of God upon the earth and which may be the beginning of the final outpouring of the Holy Ghost which is to immediately precede the coming of the Lord."[40]

Simpson's response was positive and hopeful. He was among those who saw this is as the early sprinkles of the "latter day rains," promised in Joel 2:23. Other notable Nyack professors, like Drs. Pardington and Stevens, as well as leaders, like Alfred Snead, Missionary Secretary of the Alliance, were deeply impacted by the revival, and some received the manifestation of tongues, well documented in Dr. Paul L. King's *Genuine Gold.*

However, the movement coming out of Azusa held that speaking with tongues was a key plank in the new Pentecostal platform. Dr. Simpson and others held that tongue speaking was a legitimate gift of the Holy Spirit, but believed that Scripture did not teach it to be *the* evidence of the filling of the Holy Spirit. This evidence doctrine would become the "stone of offense," (Brumback's phrase).

However, many of Simpson's colleagues took the other position, and not a few left the Alliance to join the fledgling Assemblies of God (established 1914) or other Pentecostal groups. If this was not a true split, it was a serious erosion that set the Alliance back and disrupted for several decades the aggressive growth it had been enjoying both at home and abroad.

Revival stirrings at Nyack did not occur only in the days of Dr. Simpson, nor were manifestations of the Spirit limited to those days.

> *In October 1942, Thomas Moseley, president of the Missionary Training Institute, reported that revival broke out at Nyack with A.W. Tozer speaking. A holy hush, groaning, weeping, and holy laughter were all a part of the manifestations during this moving of the Holy Spirit.*[41]

> *Several more manifestations of holy laughter took place in the Alliance during these two decades. Late Oral Roberts University professor Dr. Charles Farah, Jr., related that in the 1940s an Alliance missionary shared about his experience of holy laughter with his father Charles Farah, Sr., who was a C&MA pastor in New England.*[42] *In July 1944, The Alliance Weekly recorded an*

account of healing with holy laughter and weeping, affirming that the gifts of the Spirit are for today, and that prophecy is needed today to give special messages to rulers and Christians, yet also cautioning that the devil can produce miracles as well.[43] *In November 1953, C&MA President Shuman recounted in the Alliance Weekly about Louis Zwiemer's [pastor of the Toledo Alliance Church] experience in 1914 of receiving the baptism in the Spirit with shouting, feeling of holy fire, and holy laughter.*[44]

The point here, of course, is not to magnify the experiences, but to note that they are not weird, heretical or to be feared. When God's Spirit descends in power upon a group or individuals, He is free to manifest His presence any way He chooses. That is exactly what Paul meant in 1 Corinthians 12:11, just after the listing of nine spiritual manifestations:

But one and the same Spirit works all these things, distributing to each one individually just as He wills.

Some believers, however, would rather not have revival if it means an outbreaking of manifestations of the Spirit. They'd rather settle for lukewarm, predictable and controllable spiritless religion than to entertain the possibility that God may interrupt our comfort-zone protocol. And I believe God will never force revival on people or a church. Those who pray for revival but will accept it only on their own terms had better stop praying; it is an insult to God.

Spiritual Children Creating New Families

In his chapter entitled *The Pentecostal "Debt" to Simpson* Charles Nienkirchen enumerates many non-Alliance Pentecostal leaders whose lives and ministries were deeply impacted by A. B. Simpson. Among them were: Charles Parham (Apostolic Faith movement), Agnes Ozman, Ambrose J. Tomlinson (Church of God – Cleveland, TN), Thomas B. Barratt (European Pentecostalism), Andrew H. Argue (Canadian Pentecostalism), Alice Flower, Alice Garrigus (Pentecostal Assemblies of Newfoundland), Lilian Yeomans (LIFE Bible College), Aimee

Semple McPherson (Foursquare Gospel), and George Jeffreys (Elim – Britain).

Nienkirchen notes also the strong genetic ties of the Assemblies of God and devotes a special section in the chapter that he subtitled: *The Assemblies of God—A Case of Denominational Indebtedness.*[45] According to him, the Bible School model, the organizational structure, the Jesus-only Christocentric emphasis, the Fourfold Gospel including the teaching and practice of divine healing, the missionary consciousness and a huge part of the leadership of the Assemblies of God were direct contributions from Simpson's legacy.

Simpson's influence continued strongly in Assemblies circles for decades. Nienkirchen writes:

> *Respect for Simpson as part of the AG's spiritual heritage did not diminish with the passage of time. The Evangel (Assemblies of God magazine) indices for 1950-64 show that no less than thirty-five excerpts from his writings appeared during the period, mostly on the subject of healing and holiness. Long after a generation of AG leaders who had Alliance backgrounds had passed from the scene, an appreciation for Simpson's legacy lived on.*[46]

Brumback also graciously acknowledges the huge debt of Pentecostals and The Assemblies of God to the Alliance, citing seven major areas of their development that are directly traceable to Dr. Simpson's vision, creativity and spiritual depth. He also bemoans what he considered to be the Alliance's shortcoming in refusing the full blessing of the revival.

> *What a shame that Dr. Simpson and other Alliance leaders misunderstood the Pentecostal message! The proclamation of the New Testament experience was not a message of condemnation, but an invitation to rejoice in the restoration of this experience to His Church.... Pentecostal believers were not out to prove that their godly Alliance brethren knew nothing of the indwelling, anointing Spirit of God. They simply believed that the **full** New Testament*

*baptism in the Spirit was made manifest by the **glossolalia,** and that it was the will of God to pour out His Spirit in this manner upon all flesh.*[47]

While being alert to the continuing disagreement about the "evidence doctrine," Brumback seems to appreciate a new spirit of conciliation between the two denominations:

It should be easy to understand, therefore, why we Pentecostal believers feel so deeply indebted to Dr. Simpson and the Christian and Missionary Alliance, and why we rejoice that much of the old feeling of antagonism has disappeared.[48]

"A Seeking" Founder and a "Seek Not" Denomination

No one questions the spiritual pioneering of Dr. A. B. Simpson. Inevitably when a person achieves "celebrity" status in the Christian community, the public is eager to fully understand the individual, and to do that we invariably use existing labels and pigeonholes for our categorizing. Was Simpson Pentecostal? Would he be called Charismatic today? Was he dispensational? Ecumenical? Denominational?

One thing he was not – spiritually stagnant. Which, of course, renders any categories as inappropriate. He was a pioneer; he never stopped his spiritual pursuit long enough to fit into any box that one might label and say, "Aha, this is A. B. Simpson." Of course, he would always ascribe to the sayings that are on his and his wife Margaret's tombstone on the Nyack College campus: "Jesus Only" and "Not I But Christ."

Charles Nienkirchen seems to understand this dimension to Simpson's spiritual psyche, as evidenced in the title of his concluding chapter, *A "Seeking" Founder and a "Seek Not" Denomination.* His point is that Simpson himself would never have ascribed to the Alliance's position of "Seek Not; Forbid Not." In all honesty, Simpson did not encourage any Christian to seek the manifestation of speaking in tongues, or for that matter, to seek any particular manifestation. He was all about seeking Jesus and His fullness.

But I think the real message of Nienkirchen's concern is that Simpson, like the aged Caleb, was always ready to tackle new spiritual frontiers. The "seek not" mentality can be used to discourage any expectation of spiritual experience. Once we have told God what we will not accept in spiritual experience, we have asked Him to surrender His lordship in our life. Simpson would never do that, and there is good evidence that he continued to be open to receiving the manifestation of tongues in his final years.

A five-year hiatus in his diary occurred from 1907-1912, but when he resumed writing the diary he recorded on October 6:

> *No extraordinary manifestation of the Spirit in tongues or similar gifts has come. Many of my friends have received such manifestations, but mine has still been a life of [   ] fellowship and service. At all times my spirit has been open to God for anything He might be pleased to reveal or bestow.*[49]

Did Simpson ever question whether the decisions he made about the burgeoning Pentecostal movement were right? Not according to his diary entries. However, Brumback believes differently:

> *Nyack students who managed to see Dr. Simpson alone in his later years (and it took some managing!), declare that he manifested a deep interest in the Pentecostal Revival which he had reluctantly rejected. David McDowell reported that Simpson made this sad remark in a conversation with him in 1912: "David, I did what I thought was best, but I am afraid that I missed it." McDowell also quotes A. E. Funk as admitting in a personal conversation in 1927: "David, the Alliance missed God!" McDowell replied: "Brother Funk, God honored the Alliance by laying the baby on its doorstep. But you refused the responsibility, and now the sad thing about your statement is that it is too late now—the baby has grown up!"*[50]

Alliance people will likely bristle at comments like these, and the somewhat spurious certitude of their veracity makes it even more difficult to credit. However, the point to see is that Simpson never became entrenched in an anti-Pentecostal mindset, nor did he disavow the legitimacy of the manifestations of the Holy Spirit as evidence of Spirit-filling or baptism.

Was Schism Inevitable?

Only the sovereign Lord knows why the evangelical church has been split over the evidence doctrine. Unfortunately, Dr. Simpson, one of the most humble, spiritually minded Christian leaders of the twentieth century, found himself at the center of the debate. And the debate was inside himself as well as between his fledgling Alliance and the splinter groups that were forming after the Azusa Street Revival of 1906. On the one hand Simpson always hungered for more of the sense of God's presence, more of the filling of His Spirit. On the other hand, Simpson's understanding of Scripture would not allow him to say that speaking in tongues is the necessary and only evidence of the baptism of the Holy Spirit.

As a Christian statesman, Simpson tried to be a reconciler between the differing factions, and tried to keep peace in his own Alliance family. However, many churches and pastors opted into the Pentecostal movement.

Was such an abrupt and absolute schism inevitable? Imagine if Dr. Simpson had said to the Pentecostals, "You are right; when a person receives the baptism and filling of the Holy Spirit, God provides a manifestation to confirm that experience. Tongue speaking may be the manifestation for many, but all of the nine manifestations listed in 1 Corinthians 12 are equally valid as evidence." And then he might have said to his non-Pentecostal friends, "We need to see the validity of the idea that God gives a definite confirmation of the baptism and filling of the Holy Spirit. It may be tongues; it may be some other manifestation. But we are not left to 'take it by faith'. We may need to tarry before we receive the blessing, as the first century disciples did, but the fullness of God's Spirit in your life will be accompanied by a distinct inward working that will change you dramatically."

Quite possibly Dr. Simpson did make such an appeal, to no avail. But we have no knowledge of that. Not knowing the historical and cultural context of the church in the early twentieth century, I cannot say for sure that such words would have placated either group, but quite likely, this understanding might have brought some harmony to the splintering denomination.

The question of how Simpson would view Pentecostalism or the Charismatic movement today is moot. No one knows with certainty. My opinion is that he would continue to reject the "evidence doctrine" but might very well be open to the Charismatic movement. Indeed, little, if anything, can be found in Charismatic theology that does not fit within Alliance theology. To be sure, even parts of the Charismatic movement have drifted into excesses that Simpson would not relish, but the heart that has spawned these movements is not greatly different from the great heart for God that A. B. Simpson consistently demonstrated.

Appendix B:
Abuse of *Pneumatika* from 1 Corinthians 12-14

Pneumatika are abused when:

• I do not honor the entire Godhead: Father, Son and Holy Spirit (12:4-6)

• I deny the Spirit's sovereignty in distributing manifestations as He chooses (12:14-18)

• I act or minister independently of the rest of the body (12:14-18)

• I show more honor to the more external, obvious gifts (12:22-25)

• I expect all members to exhibit any one gift or all the gifts (12:29-30)

• I make the gifts more important than love (12:31)

• I exercise my gift without love (13:1-3)

• I encourage or allow uninterpreted tongue messages (14:5, 28)

• I am not seeking to edify the body (14:12, 17, 26)

• I give prominence to ecstasy over instruction (14:18-19)

• I am insensitive to novices or unbelievers (14:23)

• More than three speak in tongues in a meeting (14:27)

• More than one at a time speak in tongues (14:27)

• A prophet is not subject to other prophets (14:29, 32)

- Women interrupt the ministry by asking questions (14:34-35)

- Confusion reigns rather than peace and order (14:33, 40)

Endnotes

Introduction

[1] Both Hebrew (*ruach*) and Greek (*pneuma*), words for "spirit," also mean wind or breath.

[2] A. W. Tozer, *Keys to the Deeper Life* (Grand Rapids, MI: Zondervan Publishing House, 1957), p. 52.

[3] *Surprised By Joy* is the title of C. S. Lewis' most autobiographical book published in 1955.

[4] Throughout this book I will use variations on the Greek word *pneuma*, which means spirit, breath or wind. For example, pneumaphobic refers to being fearful or averse to the spirit or Spirit; pneumatic is an adjectival use of pneuma; pneumatology is the doctrine of the Holy Spirit.

[5] Here I use the term evangelical to refer to those believers and churches which espouse the historic biblical tenets of the Christian faith which include but are not limited to:

Faith in the triune God—Father, Son and Holy Spirit

Belief in the eternal existence, virgin birth, sinless life, atoning sacrifice and bodily resurrection of the Son of God, Jesus Christ

Experience of the (new) birth of the human spirit by repentance of sin, belief in Jesus Christ as Lord, and confession of salvation (John 3:16; Romans 10:9,10)

Confidence in the trustworthiness of Scripture and submission to its authority

[6] See, for example, Simpson's book, *The Holy Spirit*, written in two sections showing Old Testament and New Testament "types" of the Holy Spirit.

[7] The Great Commission is the name commonly given to Matthew 28:19, 20: *Go therefore and make disciples of all the nations, baptizing them in the name of the Father and the Son and the Holy Spirit, teaching them to observe all that I commanded you; and lo, I am with you always, even to the end of the age.*

[8] Founded in 1887 as a missionary society, The Christian and Missionary Alliance today is a global movement of denominations in approximately 50 nations, aligning itself with the evangelical segment of the Church.

Chapter One

[9] The C&MA was begun before the modern day Pentecostal movement, and eagerly embraced the spiritual gifts and manifestations, but for the past half century the pneumatology of the movement has been decidedly ambiguous. Alliance people are not sure whether they are pentegelical or evangecostal. As the Alliance moved from being a movement to being a denomination (officially declared in 1974), the theology of "Seek Not; Forbid Not" (regarding speaking in tongues) in practice became "Seek Not; Better Not" in most churches.

Chapter Two

[10] Chuck Brewster in *Momentum, volume 2, Issue 6, June 2004, a monthly publication of HonorBound: Men of Promise. Cf. www.honorbound. com.*

[11] A. B. Simpson, *The Holy Spirit* (New York, 1896), 2. 25, cited in Gerald F. Hawthorne, *The Presence and the Power (*Eugene, OR; Wipf and Stock Publishers)*, pp. 234-235.

Chapter Three

[12] The *Septuagint,* the Greek translation of the Old Testament, was translated in about 200 B.C., so it was available to those who could read Greek, but how many copies existed in the first century A.D. we do not know.

Chapter Four

[13] This is not to deny that other gifts, which are not *charismata*, are found in the church and are very important for its ministry. Examples are musical ability, hospitality, dance, financial accounting, visitation, intercession, technology expertise, etc. I would consider these to be ministries, and they may be anointed and spiritually impacting.

[14] From transcription of interview between Jane Clayson and Anne Graham Lotz on the September 13, 2001, CBS television program, *Early Show.*

[15] Guy Chevreau, *Turnings* (Tonbridge, Kent, England: Sovereign World, 2004.

[16] 1 Thessalonians 5:19-21 *Do not quench the Spirit; do not despise prophetic utterances. But examine everything carefully.*

[17] 1 Corinthians 14:32 *and the spirits of prophets are subject to prophets.*

[18] See, for example, Romans 8:23-27, 1 Corinthians 14:14-15, Ephesians 6:18.

[19] A.W. Tozer, *Worship: The Missing Jewel* (Camp Hill, PA: Christian Publications, 1992), pp. 20-21

[20] A.W. Tozer, *The Pursuit of God* (Camp Hill, PA: Christian Publications, 1982), p. 75.

Chapter Five

[21] Ronald Jones and David Schroeder, *In Pursuit of the Glory of God* (Camp Hill, PA: Christian Publications, 2004).

Chapter Six

[22] Grant McClung in "Pentecostals: The Sequel," *Christianity Today*, April 2006, p. 30.

[23] See John R. W. Stott, Baptism and Fullness: The Work of the Holy Spirit Today (Westmont, IL: InterVarsity Press, 1976).

[24] George P. Pardington, *The Crisis of the Deeper Life* (Camp Hill, PA: Christian Publications, 1991 ed.), pp. 136-138.

[25] Personal correspondence with Dr. Paul L King.

[26] A.W. Tozer, *The Counselor* (Camp Hill, PA: Christian Publications, 1993), p. 72.

Chapter Seven

[27] From a personal interview, August 19, 2004.

Appendix A

[28] A. E. Thompson, *A. B. Simpson: His Life and Work* (Harrisburg: Christian Publications, Inc., 1920 [revised edition, 1960]).

[29] A. W. Tozer, *Wingspread: A. B. Simpson: A Study in Spiritual Altitude* (Harrisburg: Christian Publications, Inc., 1943).

[30] Robert K. Nicklaus, John S. Sawin and Samuel J Stoesz, *All For Jesus* (Camp Hill, PA: Christian Publications, 1986).

[31] Daniel J. Evearitt, *Body & Soul: Evangelism and the Social Concern of A. B. Simpson* (Camp Hill, PA: Christian Publications, 1994).

[32] Charles W. Nienkirchen, *A. B. Simpson and the Pentecostal Movement* (Peabody, MA: Hendrickson Publishers, 1992).

[33] Edith L. Blumhofer, from Nienkirchen, back cover.

[34] Carl Brumback, *A Sound From Heaven* (info needed)

[35] Gary B. McGee, *Pentecostal Awakenings at Nyack*, in *Paraclete*, summer 1984.

[36] Nienkirchen, p. 9.

[37] Nienkirchen, p. 28.

[38] Quoted in Carl Brumback, p. 86.

[39] A. B. Simpson *The Tenth Annual Report of the Christian and Missionary Alliance*, pp 77, 78, cited by McGee.

[40] George N. Eldridge, *Tenth Annual Report*, cited by McGee.

[41] Thomas Moseley, "Revival at Nyack," *Alliance Weekly*, October 10, 1942, p. 643.

[42] Personal recollections of Dr. Charles Farah, Jr., concerning his father.

[43] E. Fred Page, "Gifts of Healing," *Alliance Weekly*, July 29, 1944, pp. 324-325, 336.

[44] H. M. Shuman, "Louis Henry Zweimer," *Alliance Weekly*, Nov. 4, 1953, pp. 10-11.

[45] Nienkirchen, pp. 41-51.

[46] Nienkirchen, p. 51.

[47] Brumback, p. 90.

[48] Brumback, p. 93.

[49] A. B. Simpson diary, typed from the original by Miss Alda Greely, secretary to Alliance President H. M. Shuman on November 21, 1942, and available in the C&MA Archives in Colorado Springs, CO.

[50] Brumback, personal interview with David McDowell, October 20, 1959.

INDEX

Scriptures

150

A

Adenuga, Paul Taiwo 65
Anderson, Gordon 59
Argue, Andrew H. 137

B

Bailey, Richard W. 15
Baker, Roland and Heidi 62
Barratt, Thomas B. 137
Blumhofer, Edith 132, 133
Boardman, William E. 133
Bosworth 100
Brumback, Carl 132, 134, 136, 138,
    139, 140, 148
Bubna, Paul iii, 14, 91

C

Cannon, George 85
Clayson, Jane 56, 146
Coffey, Roland 11
Cox, Herbert 134

D

Davey, James E. 7

E

Edman, V. Raymond 125
Eldredge, John 21
Eldridge, George N. 135, 148
Evearitt, Daniel J. 132, 147

F

Farah, Charles 136, 148
Flower, Alice 137
Funk, A.E. 114, 140

G

Garrigus, Alice 137
Gibbs, Eddie 105
Gothard, Bill 14
Graham, Billy 56
Green, Michael 14

J

Jeffreys, George 138
Jones, Ron 91

K

Kenyon, Paul 7
King, Paul L. vi, 100

L

Larsen, Fran 87
Lewis, C.S. 1, 11, 145
Lotz, Anne Graham 56, 146

M

Manning, Brennan 21
Mason, C.J. 7
McDowell, David 140
McGee, Gary B. 132, 135, 148
McPherson, Aimee Semple 137
Miller, Tracey 7
Morley, Patrick 21
Moseley, Thomas 136, 148
Motessi, Alberto 15

N

Nicklaus, Robert K. 132, 147
Nienkirchen, Charles 132, 133, 134,
    137, 138, 139, 140, 147, 148
Norman, Larry 63
Nouwen, Henri 21

O

Olford, Stephen 9
Ozman, Agnes 137

P

Palmer, Phoebe 100
Pardington, George 98, 136, 147
Parham, Charles 137
Pawson, David 14, 39

R

Roberts, Evans 134

S

Sawin, John S. 132, 147
Schaeffer, Francis 11
Seymour, William J. 96, 100
Shuman, President 137
Simpson, Albert Benjamin ix, xiii, 2,
      6, 7, 10, 15, 16, 17, 100, 131,
      132, 133, 134, 136, 137, 138,
      139, 140, 141, 142, 145, 146,
      147, 148
Smith, Chuck 15, 87
Smith, Hannah Whitall 100
Snead, Alfred 136
Stanley, Charles 87
Stevens, W. C. 135
Stoesz, Samuel J. 132
Swindoll, Chuck 87

T

Tomlinson, Ambrose J. 137
Tozer, A.W. 69, 107, 136, 147
Tson, Joseph 15

W

Walker, Harold 9
Watson, David 14
Willard, Dallas 19, 20
Wilson, Roy 8

Y

Yeomans, Lilian 137

Z

Zwiemer, Louis 137